U1074791

round your bed Right next to your bed Trying to understand Closer closer closer

... If I had my wishes If I had my way I'd be all the world to you Each and every

While I'm on ... Changing to ... days Everywhere you move around I ...

closer closer to you Closer get to get closer closer to you If I were a piece of ...

satisfied Just being around you by When I am dreaming Wishes a ...

decorate your lips Closer closer closer to you Closer get to get closer closer to you

Close your eyes When you feel the time was right I'll ... what you want While

As You Like It

莎翁戏剧经典

皆大欢喜

〔英〕威廉·莎士比亚　著
罗志野　李德荣　注释

商務印書館
SINCE 1897
The Commercial Press
2016年·北京

威廉·莎士比亚

图 1

图 2（见 6 页）

ORL. … This is it, Adam, that grieves
me; and the spirit of my father, which I think is within me, begins to mutiny against this servitude. I will no longer endure it, though yet I know no wise remedy how to avoid it.

图 3（见 8 页）

OLI. Wilt thou lay hands on me villain?

ORL. I am no villain; I am the youngest son of Sir Rowland de Boys; he was my father, and he is thrice a villain that says such a father begot villains.

图 4（见 16 页）

ROS. From henceforth I will, coz, and devise sports. Let me see; what think you of falling in love?

CEL. Marry, I prithee, do, to make sport withal: but love no man in good earnest; nor no further in sport, neither, than with safety of a pure blush thou mayst in honour come off again.

图 5（见 44—46 页）

DUKE S. Come, shall we go and kill us venison? And yet it irks me, the poor dappled fools,
Being native burghers of this desert city,
Should in their own confines with forked heads
Have their round haunches gor'd.

First Lord. … and, indeed, my lord,
The wretched animal heav'd forth such groans
That their discharge did stretch his leathern coat
Almost to bursting, and the big round tears
…
In piteous chase…

图 6（见 58 页）

SIL. If thou remember'st not the slightest folly
That ever love did make thee run into,
Thou hast not lov'd:
Or if thou hast not sat as I do now,
Wearing thy hearer with thy mistress' praise,
Thou hast not lov'd:
Or if thou hast not broke from company
Abruptly, as my passion now makes me,
Thou hast not lov'd.

图 7（见 84—86 页）

ORL. Hang there, my verse, in witness of my love:
And thou, thrice-crowned queen of night, survey With
thy chaste eye, from thy pale sphere above,
Thy huntress' name, that my full life doth sway.

图 8（见 112 页）

AUD. I do not know what 'poetical' is. Is it honest in deed and word? Is it a true thing?

TOUCH. No, truly, for the truest poetry is the most feigning; and lovers are given to poetry, and what they swear in poetry may be said as lovers they do feign.

图 9（见 132 页）

ROS. They say you are a melancholy fellow.

JAQ. I am so; I do love it better than laughing.

ROS. Those that are in extremity of either are abominable fellows, and betray themselves to every modern censure worse than drunkards.

图 10（见 162 页）

WILL. Ay, sir, I have a pretty wit.

TOUCH. Why, thou sayest well. I do now remember a saying, 'The fool doth think he is wise, but the wise man knows himself to be a fool.'

图 11（见 190 页）

ROS. … O women! for the love
you bear to men, to like as much of this play as please
you: and I charge you, O men! for the love you bear to
women, —as I perceive by your simpering none of
you hate them, —that between you and the women, the
play may please.

“莎翁戏剧经典”丛书总序

莎士比亚（William Shakespeare，1564—1616）是英国16世纪文艺复兴时期的伟大剧作家和诗人，也是世界文坛上的巨擘。他一生创作了38部戏剧作品（一说37部），诗作包括两部长篇叙事诗、一部十四行诗集以及其他一些短篇诗作。四百多年来这些作品被翻译成多种文字，在世界各地广泛传播。正如他同时代的批评家和剧作家本·琼生所说，他是“时代的灵魂”，“不属一个时代，而属于所有的时代！”莎士比亚在世期间，他的戏剧作品曾吸引了大量观众，包括宫廷王室成员和普通百姓，产生了巨大影响。18世纪以来，这些作品始终活跃在舞台上，20世纪随着电影业的发展，它们又被搬上银幕。几百年来，无论是体现莎士比亚原作的表演还是经过不断改编的作品，莎剧都拥有众多的观者，散发出不灭的艺术光辉；另一方面，自1623年莎士比亚全集第一对开本问世，莎士比亚的戏剧也成为学者和广大普通读者阅读、学习、研究的对象，在历代读者的阅读和研究中，这些作品不断得到新阐释和挖掘。莎士比亚的作品焕发着永久不衰的生命活力。

1564年4月，莎士比亚出生于英格兰中部的埃文河畔的斯特拉福镇。家境殷实，父亲曾经营手套和羊毛，并做过小镇的镇长。莎士比亚小时曾在镇上的文法学校读书，受到过较为正规的拉丁文和古典文学的教育。不久，家道中落，陷入经济困境，这可能成为莎士比亚后来未能进入大学读书的原因。1582年，莎士比亚十八岁时与邻村一位大他八岁的女子安·哈撒韦成婚，六个月后，大女儿苏珊娜降生，此后他们又有了一对孪生子女，不幸的是，儿子哈姆内特早夭。16世纪90年代左右，莎士比亚来到伦敦，发展他的戏剧事业。他曾是剧团的演员、编剧和股东。90年代初期，莎士比亚即开始戏剧创作。1592年，莎士比亚已在同行中崭露头角，被当时的“大学才子”剧作家格林所嫉妒，他把莎士比亚称作“那只新抖起来的乌鸦”，“借我们的羽毛来打扮自己……狂妄地幻想着能独自震撼(Shake-scene)这个国家的舞台”。1592—1594年间，伦敦因流行瘟疫，大部分剧院关闭，在此期间莎士比亚完成了两部著名的长篇叙事诗《维纳斯与阿多尼斯》与《鲁克丽丝受辱记》。1594年剧院恢复营业之后，莎士比亚加入宫廷大臣剧团，并终生服务于该剧团，直到1613年离开伦敦返回家乡。90年代中期，他进入了戏剧创作的巅峰时期。在1590年至1613年的二十多年之间，莎士比亚共创作了历史剧、悲剧、喜剧、传奇剧等38部。90年代中后期，他的创作以喜剧和历史剧为主，包括喜剧《仲夏夜之梦》(1595)、《威尼斯商人》(1596)、《无事生非》(1598—1599)、《皆大欢喜》(1599—1600)等和大部分历史剧，如《理查三世》(1592—1593)、《亨利四世》(上、下)(1596—1598)、《亨利五世》(1598—1599)等。这一时期，他的创作风格较为明快，充满积极向上的格调，即便剧中有悲剧的成分，整个作品也透露出对生活的肯定，对理想的向往，如《罗密欧与朱丽叶》(1595)。进入17世纪后，莎士比亚的戏剧更多地转向对人生重大问题的思考，探索解决人生之困顿的途径，诸如权力、欲望、嫉妒、暴政等等。四大悲剧《哈姆莱特》(1600—1601)、《奥瑟罗》(1603—1604)、《李尔王》(1605—1606)、《麦克白》(1606)均完成于这一时期。此外，几部重要的罗马题材剧也在90年代末和新世纪的最初几年完成，如《裘力·凯撒》(1599)、《安东尼与克里奥佩特拉》(1606)、《科里奥兰纳斯》(1608)等。莎士比亚这一时期也创作了几部喜剧，但风格较前一时期更多悲情色彩，更为沉重而引人深思。1609年，莎士比亚《十四行诗集》出版。晚期的莎士比亚剧作风格有一定变化，最有影响的是传奇剧，如《暴风雨》，通过想象的世界与现实世界的对照来探讨人生问题。

莎士比亚的名字开始传入中国是在19世纪中上叶，他的戏剧被翻译成汉语而为国人所知则是在20世纪初期。当时，他剧作的内容通过英国19世纪兰姆姐弟《莎士比亚戏剧故事集》的汉译被介绍到中国来，即无译者署名的《澥外奇谭》(1903)和林纾、魏易翻译的《吟边燕语》(1904)。20 世纪 20 年代，莎剧汉译事业的开拓者田汉翻译了《哈孟雷特》(1921)和《罗密欧与朱丽叶》(1924)。此后，朱生豪、梁实秋、孙大雨、曹禺、曹未风、虞尔昌等译家都翻译过莎士比亚的剧作。朱生豪先生在经历日本侵略的苦难、贫穷和疾病折磨的极其艰苦的环境下，以惊人的毅力和顽强的意志，克服种种艰难险阻，穷毕生之精力完成了 31 部半莎剧的翻译，成为播撒莎士比亚文明之火的普罗米修斯，译莎事业的英雄和圣徒。他的莎剧译文优美畅达，人物性格鲜明，成为广大读者所珍爱的艺术瑰宝。梁实秋是中国迄今为止唯一一位个人独立完成莎剧和莎诗汉译工程的翻译家。梁译有详尽的注释和说明，学术含量较高。1956 年，卞之琳翻译的《哈姆雷特》出版，他完善了孙大雨提出的翻译原则，提出“以顿代步、韵式依原诗、等行翻译”的翻译方法，可谓开一代诗体译法之风，他的译本至今都被视作该剧最优秀的译本。方平是另一位重要的成绩卓著的莎剧翻译家。2000 年由他主编主译的《新莎士比亚全集》出版，其中 25 部莎剧由方平翻译，其他作品由阮坤、吴兴华、汪义群、覃学岚、屠岸、张冲等译出，为国内目前首部全部由分行诗体翻译的莎剧莎诗全集。

时至今日，莎士比亚的戏剧作品仍不断有新的译本出版，对广大读者而言，阅读汉译的莎剧已经是一件十分方便的事情，而这些汉译莎剧作品中不乏优秀的译本。然而，尽管莎剧的汉译丰富多彩，莎剧的改编层出不穷，要想真正了解莎剧的本来面目，我们还须要回到莎剧原文本身。其中的原因有三：一、每一种语言都是丰富的，其表达的意义可能是多元多面的，但由于译出语和译入语两种语言之间的差异，再好的翻译也只能尽可能地贴近原文而不可能百分之百地再现原文的魅力，因此，阅读再好的译本也无法取代或等同于阅读原作；二、莎士比亚生活的时代距今已经有约 400 年，他所使用的英语与今天人们所熟悉的英语已有较大差异，当时的人们所熟悉的文化和历史事件也是我们今天并不熟知的，因此，要真正领悟他的作品，还须回到他那时的语言和文化中去；三、莎剧经过约400年的变迁，在改编中不断变换，有些已经走出了莎士比亚时代的莎剧，因而，想要认识和了解莎剧，最佳的办法还是回到莎剧的原文本中去。

莎士比亚生活和创作的时期在16世纪末17世纪初。英语在当时已经得到极大的发展，十分活跃而成熟，尤其莎士比亚戏剧中所运用的英语，文辞丰富、结构灵活、表达力很强。但随着时代的发展，其中的一些用词、用语以及语义等都发生了变化，与我们今天的英语存在一定距离，理解起来也就会有一定困难。莎剧在绝大多数情况下采用的是诗体写作，即人物的语言是分行的，每行十个音节，轻重音节相间，一轻一重的每两个音节构成一个音步，不押韵，因此，他的剧作均为抑扬格五音步的素体诗。这样的诗体形式突显出莎剧语言的艺术魅力，音韵优美、铿锵，节奏感强，表达生动有力。然而，正因为这是诗体写作，在语法上就可能出现诗语言特有的结构，比如倒装句或词序颠倒的现象等。莎剧的语言丰富多彩，不同人物的话语呈现出多种特色，时而体现出古典拉丁语的文风，时而出现双关语、俚语、隐喻等修辞手法。典故、历史事件、政治元素、宗教、生活习俗等等都可能成为今天的读者理解莎剧原文本的障碍。因而，借助良好的注释来理解莎剧的原作就成为我们了解和认识莎剧原貌的必要手段。这次由商务印书馆隆重推出的“莎翁戏剧经典”丛书，重点选出莎士比亚的12部经典剧作，在裘克安先生主编的“莎士比亚注释”丛书的基础上进行了改编修订，并加入了精美的插图。裘先生主编的“莎士比亚注释”丛书对莎剧原文做了多方面的详尽注释，对理解原文起到有效作用，在读者中有较广泛的影响。相信这套“莎翁戏剧经典”的出版会进一步推动莎剧在广大读者中的影响力，提高人们对阅读莎剧以及经典文学作品原文的兴趣和能力，产生积极的和广泛的影响。

屠岸 章燕

2013年10月4日

“莎士比亚注释”丛书总序

莎士比亚研究在新中国有过不平坦的道路和坎坷的命运。解放后不久，大家纷纷学俄语，学英语的人数骤减。研究英国文学，要看苏联人怎么说。“文革”十年，莎士比亚同其他西方“资产阶级”作家一样被打入冷宫。改革开放以后，1978年人民文学出版社出版了在朱生豪译文基础上修订补足的《莎士比亚全集》。随之又出版了一些个别剧的不同译本，如方平译的《莎士比亚喜剧五种》(1979年)和卞之琳译的《莎士比亚悲剧四种》(1988年)。梁实秋的译本，现在大陆上也可以读到了。评介和研究莎士比亚的文章，从“文革”结束后才逐渐多起来。

但是，目前多数人学习、欣赏和研究莎士比亚，是通过中译文来进行的。精通英语而研究莎士比亚的学者不是没有，然而他们人数不多，年纪却老迈了。最近若干年，才有一些年轻人到英国或美国去学习和研究莎士比亚。

1981年我就想到有必要在中国出版我们自己注释的莎士比亚著作。谈起来，许多朋友都赞成。1984年中国莎士比亚研究会筹备和成立时，我自告奋勇，联系了一些志同道合的学者，共同开始编写莎士比亚注释本。商务印书馆大力支持出版这套丛书。到2002年底已出书26种，而且第一次印刷版已全部售完。这证明这套丛书是很受欢迎的。

要知道，莎士比亚是英语文学中最优秀的代表人物，他又是英语语言大师，学习、欣赏和研究他的原著，是译文无法替代的。商务印书馆以其远见卓识，早在1910年和1921—1935年间，就出版过几种莎士比亚剧本的注释本，以满足这方面的需求。那时的教会学校学生英文水平高，能读莎著；不但大学生能读，连有些中学生都能读。可从那时以后，整整50年中国就没印过原文的莎士比亚著作。

世界各国，莎著的注释本多得不计其数。如果唯独中国没有，实在说不过去。如果没有，对于中国知识分子欣赏和研究莎士比亚十分不利。近年来，中国人学英语的越来越多了，他们的英文水平也逐渐提高了。因此，也存在着一定的读者市场。

有了注释本，可以为明天的莎士比亚研究提供一个可靠的群众基础。而译本显然不能提供可靠的基础。

莎士比亚是16、17世纪之交的作者，他写的又是诗剧。对于现代的读者，他的英语呈现着不少的困难。不要说掌握了现代英语的中国读者，就是受过一般教育的英美人士，在初读莎士比亚原著时也面临许多障碍，需要注释的帮助。

莎士比亚的时代，英语正从受屈折变化拘束的中世纪英语，向灵活而丰富的现代英语转变。拉丁语和法语当时对英语影响很大。而莎士比亚对英语的运用又有许多革新和创造。主要的困难可以归纳为以下几个方面，也就是注释要提供帮助的方面：

（一）词汇。许多词虽然拼法和现在一样，但具有不同的早期含义，不能望文生义。另有一些词拼法和现在不一样，而含义却相同。莎士比亚独创了一些词。他特别喜欢用双关语，在他创作的早期尤其如此。而双关语是无从翻译的。这是译本无论如何也代替不了注释本的原因之一。

让我们举《哈姆莱特》剧中男主角出场后最初讲的几句话为例：

King: But now, my cousin Hamlet, and my son —
Hamlet 〔Aside〕: A little more than kin, and less than kind!
King: How is it that the clouds still hang on you?
Hamlet: Not so, my lord. I am too much i' the sun.

• 梁实秋的译文如下：

王：现在，我的侄子哈姆雷特，也是我的儿子，——
哈[旁白]：比侄子是亲些，可是还算不得儿子。
王：怎么，你脸上还是罩着一层愁云？
哈：不是的，陛下；我受的阳光太多了。

• 卞之琳的译文如下：

王：得，哈姆雷特，我的侄子，我的儿——

哈[旁白]：亲上加亲，越亲越不相亲！

王：你怎么还是让愁云惨雾罩着你？

哈：陛下，太阳大，受不了这个热劲"儿"。

• 朱生豪的译文如下：

王：可是来，我的侄儿哈姆莱特，我的孩子——

哈[旁白]：超乎寻常的亲族，漠不相干的路人。

王：为什么愁云依旧笼罩在你的身上？

哈：不，陛下；我已经在太阳里晒得太久了。

这里，主要困难在于莎士比亚让哈姆莱特使用了 kin 和 kind 以及 son 和 sun 两组双关语。kind 一词又有双关意义，翻译无法完全表达，只能各译一个侧面。结果，梁和卞两先生还得用注释补足其义，朱译则连注释也没有。这种地方，能读原文注释本的人才能充分领略莎氏原意。

哈姆莱特在旁白里说：比亲戚多一点——本来我是你的侄子，现在又成了你的儿子，确实不是一般的亲戚关系啊；然而却比 kind 少一点——kind 有两层意思，一是"同类相求"的亲近感，一是"与人为善"的善意感，我同你没有共同语言，我也不知道你是安的什么心。这话只能对自己说，在舞台上假定对方是听不到的。哈姆莱特的第二句话是公开的俏皮话：哪里有什么阴云呀，我在太阳里晒得不行呢。sun 是跟 clouds 相对；太阳又意味着国王的恩宠，"你对我太好了，我怎么会阴郁呢？"sun 又跟 son 谐音，"做你的儿子，我领教得够了。"原文并不是像梁实秋所说的那样晦涩难解。可是含义太复杂，有隐藏的深层感情，所以无法译得完全。

（二）语法。有些现象，按现代英语语法的标准看，似乎是错误的，但在当时并不错，是属于中世纪英语的残余因素。例如有些动词过去分词的词尾变化、代词的所有格形式、主谓语数的不一致、关系代词和介词的用法等方面，都有一些和现在不同的情况。注释里说明了，可以举一反三去理解。

（三）词序的颠倒和穿插。词尾屈折变化较多的中世纪英语本来对词序没有严格的要求。伊丽莎白时代继承了这种习惯。同时,诗的节律和押韵要求对词序作一定的灵活处理。莎士比亚的舞台语言以鲜明、有力、生动为首要考虑,有时他就把语法和句法放在从属的地位。在激动的台词中,由于思路、感情的变化,语言也常有脱出常规的变化。这些地方,有了注释的指点,理解就容易得多。

(四)典故。莎士比亚用典很多。古希腊、罗马神话,《圣经》故事,英国民间传说,历史逸事……他都随手拈来。其中有一大部分对于英美读者来说乃是常识,但中国读者就很需要注释的帮助。

(五)文化背景。注释可以提供关于基督教义、中世纪传统观点、文艺复兴时期新的主张、英国习俗等方面的知识。

除上述以外,还有莎剧中影射时事,以及版本考据诸问题,在注释本中可以详细论述,也可以简单提及。

世界文豪莫不是语言大师,而要真正理解和欣赏一位大师的文笔,当然非读他的原著不成。出版莎士比亚注释本,首先是为了让中国读者便于买到和读到他的原著。不过我们自知现出的几十种在版本、注释和其他方面还存在不足之处,希望读者多提意见,以便今后不断改进。

裘克安

前　　言

莎士比亚的《皆大欢喜》是一出著名的喜剧。出版该文原著的注释本，目的在于帮助我国的读者能从原著来欣赏作品的深层意义及伊丽莎白时代的英国书面语言的特色。

威廉·莎士比亚(1564—1616)是欧洲文艺复兴时期最有成就的诗人和剧作家之一。他生活的时代正值伊丽莎白一世及詹姆士一世的统治时期。莎士比亚出身于英国中部斯特拉福城一个富裕市民的家庭，少年时代曾在当地的文法学校读书，学习修辞、逻辑及拉丁文等。22 岁时离开自己的故乡，去到繁荣的首都伦敦谋生，寻找机会，广泛接触各阶层的生活，加深了对社会的认识。1590 年左右，他进了剧团，开始了舞台与创作生活。如在第 110 首十四行诗中他写道：

“我曾经走遍各地，
让自己在世人面前穿上彩衣，
割裂思想，廉价售出最贵重的东西。”

莎士比亚在剧团时，既要参加演出，又要进行创作，有时还要参加巡回演出，如在第 22 首十四行诗中他说：

“劳动使我疲倦了，我急忙上床，
来好好安歇我旅途劳累的四肢；
但是脑子里的旅行又旋即开场，
劳力刚刚完毕，劳心却又开始。”

莎士比亚的绝大部分戏剧都是通过对现成材料的改编与加工而完成的。在 20 多年中，他一共写了 39 部戏剧，两首长诗，154 首十四行诗，以及一些杂诗。1613 年才离开伦敦回到久别的故乡。1616 年逝世。

《皆大欢喜》是莎士比亚创作第一时期中的重要喜剧之一。莎士比亚采用“皆大欢喜”这个剧名，是根据托马斯·劳基

(1558—1625)的一篇《罗瑟琳》的小说,其中有"If you like it"的话,莎士比亚便拿来改为"As You Like It"。故事的内容早在14世纪就产生了,当时流传着《盖尼米德的故事》,不过经过莎士比亚的改写后,喜剧的色彩得到光辉的发扬,人物的性格更加鲜明。

《皆大欢喜》是一出五幕喜剧,约创作于1598—1600年间,写好后就上演。当时莎士比亚35岁左右。直到目前还没有发现有过四开本的原著,就现在的资料所知,第一次对开本是1623年出版的,而且在1600年左右是为英国人民所欢迎的流行剧之一。

这部喜剧的剧情大致是这样的:在一个无名的国度里,弗莱德里克把他的哥哥(一位合法的公爵)流放了,自己取而代之。公爵带着追随者住到亚登森林。公爵的女儿罗瑟琳留在宫中,和弗莱德里克的女儿西莉娅做伴。

另外,鲍埃爵士有三个儿子,死前托大儿子奥列佛照料两个弟弟贾奎斯和奥兰多。奥列佛虐待奥兰多,使他成人后一未受教育,二无钱财。同时还恨他,唆使他与弗莱德里克的拳师比武,希望奥兰多在比武中丧生。结果奥兰多获胜,并且和罗瑟琳相互爱慕。

弗莱德里克不久又流放罗瑟琳,她去森林寻父,西莉娅愿意同往,为了便于寻找父亲,不惹麻烦,罗瑟琳女扮男装,改名盖尼米德。

奥兰多得到消息,说奥列佛正设计陷害他,他只有带着老仆人也进入莽莽森林。在路上他遇到了罗瑟琳,由于她化了装,又改了名,所以没有认出。

奥兰多想念罗瑟琳,罗瑟琳决定试探一下他,看他是否真心。

不久,奥列佛也被流放,在森林中遇到毒蛇与母狮,眼看他就要丧生,正巧奥兰多走来,他不记前仇,赶走动物,自己受伤。奥列佛感谢弟弟救他,便转恨为爱。接着奥列佛爱上了西莉娅。后来他们四人一起找到了公爵,得到公爵的允许,罗瑟琳与奥兰多、西莉娅与奥列佛结婚。

弗莱德里克决定率领军队开赴森林，消灭公爵及其追随者。但是在森林中，他遇到了一位智慧的隐士，劝他放弃统治，诚心皈依宗教。这样，他回心转意，请公爵回国治理政务。

这部喜剧盘绕着一条主线，一是公爵被弗莱德里克流放；二是罗瑟琳与西莉娅被流放；三是奥兰多受虐待，逃进森林。所谓“皆大欢喜”是指被流放的人都得到善的结局，公爵复位，有情的人全成眷属。而恶人在受到谆谆教诲后也改过自新。

喜剧表现出一个乌托邦的理想世界，这个理想世界中，道德显示出巨大的力量，恶人能受到感化，大家知恩能报，善良的人最后有善终；爱情纯朴，一见钟情。无疑，这是莎士比亚所理想的境界，他希望善能战胜恶，他期求纯直与幸福，从而把这种理想与现实之中的虚伪友谊、轻佻爱情、尔虞我诈、不容良善的情况作实际的对比。

莎士比亚的书面语言丰富多彩，但今天的人阅读时却可能产生一些麻烦，同样的词根，而含义可能不同；还可能拼写不同，比如下面有一些词是常遇到的：

原文	今文	原文	今文
an	if	ere	before
ay	yes	methinks	it seems to me
become	suit		(that)
coz	cousin	nay	no
prithee	please	ta'en	taken
sooth	truth	ron	yond
spake	spoke		

这仅是几个例子，更多的在注释中出现，请读者随时注意。

除词汇外，《皆大欢喜》中存在着许多值得欣赏与学习的修辞现象。如明喻方面有：

Sweet are the uses of adversity,
Which, like the toad, ugly and venomous,
Wears yet a precious jewel in his head

隐喻方面有：

All the world's a stage,
And all the men and women merely players:
They have their exits and their entrances,
And one man in his time plays many parts

拟人化方面有：

Though Nature hath given us wit to flout at
Fortune, hath not
Fortune sent in this fool to cut off the argument?

在语法方面，按现在英语语法的标准看，有些句子似乎是错的，而在当时却是对的，如主谓语数的不一致性、动词过去分词用了过去式等。这些方面在阅读时该留心。

莎士比亚时代的舞台言语以鲜明、有力、生动为主，而语法却处于次要地位。因为在激动的台词中，由于思路与情感的变化，语言也常会有脱出常规的变化。

本书注释采各家之长，尽量做到读之易懂，简明确切。读者借助注释再下些功夫，是可以读懂原著的。遇到一些考据中的疑难问题，读者可以不必探究，因为这需要大量的资料与工具书。

对于注释的不足之处，希望读者指出，以便再版时改进。

罗志野
于江西大学

AS YOU LIKE IT

DRAMATIS PERSONAE

DUKE, *living in exile.*

FREDERICK, *his Brother, usurper of his dominions.*

AMIENS,
JAQUES, } *lords attending upon the banished Duke.*

LE BEAU, *a courtier, attending upon Frederick.*

CHARLES, *a wrestler to Frederick.*

OLIVER,
JAQUES,
ORLANDO, } *sons of Sir Rowland de Boys.*

ADAM,
DENNIS, } *servants to Oliver.*

TOUCHSTONE, *a clown.*

SIR OLIVER MARTEXT, *a vicar.*

CORIN,
SILVIUS, } *shepherds.*

WILLIAM, *a country fellow, in love with Audrey.*

A person representing Hymen.

ROSALIND, *daughter to the banished Duke.*

CELIA, *daughter to Frederick.*

PHEBE, *a shepherdess.*

AUDREY, *a country wench.*

LORDS, PAGES, FORESTERS, *and* ATTENDANTS.

注　　释

1 **Dramatis Personae**〈拉丁语〉：character of the drama，剧中人物。

2 人物名字读音：

Frederick [ˈfredrik]

Amiens [əˈmjiənz]

Jaques [ˈdʒeik(w)iz]

Le Beau [ləˈbɔː]，可能是法国人。

Orlando [ɔːˈlɑːndəu]

Martext [ˈmɑːtekst]

Corin [ˈkɔrin]

Silvius [ˈsilviəs]

Rosalind [ˈrəusəlind]

Celia [ˈsiːliə]

Phebe [fiːb]

Audrey [ˈɔːdri]

3 **Dominions**：(封建时代王公贵族的)领地。

4 **Hymen** [ˈhaimən]：希腊罗马神话中司人间婚姻之神。

SCENE.—*First*, OLIVER'S *Orchard near his House; afterwards, in the Usurper's Court, and in the Forest of Arden.*

ACT I

SCENE I

—*An Orchard near* OLIVER'S *House.*

Enter ORLANDO *and* ADAM.

ORL.

As I remember, Adam, it was upon this fashion bequeathed me by will but poor a thousand crowns, and, as thou sayest, charged my brother, on his blessing, to breed me well: and there begins my sadness. My brother Jaques he keeps at school, and report speaks goldenly of his profit: for my part, he keeps me rustically at home, or, to speak more properly, stays me here at home unkept; for call you that keeping for a gentleman of my birth, that differs not from the stalling of an ox? His horses are bred better; for, besides that they are fair with their feeding, they are taught their manage, and to that end riders dearly hired: but I, his brother, gain nothing under him but growth; for the which his animals on his dunghills are as much bound to him as I. Besides this nothing that he so plentifully gives me, the something that nature gave me, his countenance seems to take from

I.i（第一幕第一场，后类推）（以下黑体数字为行码）

开场时，已故 Rowland 爵士的幼子 Orlando 在和仆人 Adam 谈论 Rowland 的遗嘱等问题。

1—2 upon this fashion：in this way. **bequeathed** 前省略了 that he，即 Orlando 的父亲 Sir Rowland. 下行中 charged 的主语同此。 **by will**：by his will，在遗嘱中。 **but**：only. **poor a**：a mere，a miserable.

2—3 crowns：一个 crown 值四分之一英镑。 **thou**：旧时指第二人称单数代词主格，宾格是 thee，所有格是 thy，thine. 其动词末尾一般为-st. 当时一般下对上称 you，上对下称 thou；对疏远者称 you，对亲者称 thou. 这里是小主人对仆人称 thou.

3—4 on his blessing：as a condition for receiving his (their father's) blessing. **breed**：educate.

4 my brother：指大哥 Oliver，根据英国法律，长子继承全部财产。

4—5 My brother Jaques：二哥。 **school**：university. **report**：common talk. **goldenly**：excellently.

6 profit：progress. **rustically**：like a rustic（乡下人）。

7—8 stays...unkept：留在家里，养而不教。stays 意为 retains，unkept 意为 uneducated. **call you**：do you call，旧时只要把主谓语颠倒，即可构成疑问句。

7—10 that differs not...：系上行中 that 的定语从句。differs not 等于 does not differ. **stalling**：stabling，关在牛圈里。

10 fair with：in good condition because of.

11 manage：（n. 从意大利语 maneggio）training of a riding horse in its paces. **to...end**：for that purpose. **riders**：experts in horse-training. **riders dearly hired**：hired riders at great expense，原文倒装。

12—13 but：except. **for the which**：for which. 在古英语中 which 为名词，前可加冠词。

13 bound：indebted.

15 plentifully：generously. **something**：special quality.

16 countenance：treatment (of me).

me: he lets me feed with his hinds, bars me the place of a brother, and, as much as in him lies, mines my gentility with my education. This is it, Adam, that grieves me; and the spirit of my father, which I think is within me, begins to mutiny against this servitude. I will no longer endure it, though yet I know no wise remedy how to avoid it.

ADAM. Yonder comes my master, your brother.

ORL. Go apart, Adam, and thou shalt hear how he will shake me up.

Enter OLIVER

OLI. Now, sir! what make you here?

ORL. Nothing: I am not taught to make anything.

OLI. What mar you then, sir?

ORL. Marry, sir, I am helping you to mar that which God made, a poor unworthy brother of yours, with idleness.

OLI. Marry, sir, be better employed, and be naught awhile.

ORL. Shall I keep your hogs and eat husks with them? What prodigal portion have I spent, that I should come to such penury?

OLI. Know you where your are, sir?

ORL. O! sir, very well: here in your orchard.

OLI. Know you before whom, sir?

ORL. Ay, better than he I am before knows me. I know you are my eldest brother; and, in the gentle condition of blood, you should so know me. The courtesy of nations allows you my better, in that you are the first-born; but the same tradition takes not away my blood, were there twenty brothers betwixt us. I have as much of my father in me as you; albeit, I confess, your coming before me is nearer to his reverence.

18 hinds: farm labourers. **bars**: denies.

19—20 as...lies: doing as much as he can. **mines**: undermines. **gentility**: noble birth. **with...education**: by bringing me up like this.

22 mutiny(v.): revolt. **servitude**: state of being a servant.

27 shake...up: abuse me.

28 what make you: what are you doing."make"更为普通的意思是"制作",下行中的 Orlando 即以此义与其兄打诨。

30 mar: spoil,damage.make 和 mar 是对义语。

31 Marry: by the Virgin Mary(轻微赌咒语)。参看 Idleness spoils a child. **that**: the one.

34—35 be naught: make yourself scarce. **awhile**: for a while.

36—38 Shall...penury: 典出《圣经·新约·路加福音》第 15 章第 11—16 节,讲一个放荡的小儿子在耗尽父亲分给他的产业后,为人放猪,只能以猪食充饥。 **hogs**: pigs. **husks**: (猪吃的)糠食。**prodigal portion**: big inheritance (of the Prodigal Sea). **spent**: wasted. **penury**: poverty.

39 你知道你在对谁说话? Orlando 下行回答时佯装不懂。

40 orchard: 花园。

42 better...me: 我知道我面前的人,比我面前的人知道我要清楚得多。I am before 是 he(有的版本作 him)的定语。

43—44 in...blood: 以高尚血统的人应有的情感而言。

45 courtesy of nations: custom of the civilized world. **allows...better**: acknowledges your authority over me.

47 blood: breeding. **betwixt**: between.

48 albeit: though.

49 nearer to his reverence: entitled to more of the respect due to him.

OLI. What, boy!

ORL. Come, come, elder brother, you are too young in this.

OLI. Wilt thou lay hands on me villain?

ORL. I am no villain; I am the youngest son of Sir Rowland de Boys; he was my father, and he is thrice a villain that says such a father begot villains. Wert thou not my brother, I would not take this hand from thy throat till this other had pulled out thy tongue for saying so: thou hast railed on thyself.

Adam. [*Coming forward*.] Sweet masters, be patient: for your father's remembrance, be at accord.

OLI. Let me go, I say.

ORL. I will not, till I please: you shall hear me. My father charged you in his will to give me good education: you have trained me like a peasant, obscuring and hiding from me all gentleman-like qualities. The spirit of my father grows strong in me, and I will no longer endure it: therefore allow me such exercises as may become a gentleman , or give me the poor allottery my father left me by testament; with that I will go buy my fortunes.

OLI. And what wilt thou do? beg, when that is spent? Well, sir, get you in: I will not long be troubled with you; you shall have some part of your will: I pray you, leave me.

ORL. I will no further offend you than becomes me for my good.

OLI. Get you with him, you old dog.

ADAM. Is 'old dog' my reward? Most true, I have lost my teeth in your service. God be with my old master! he would not have spoke such a word.

[*Exeunt* ORLANDO *and* ADAM.

50 称大人 boy，是侮辱之词。说此话时 Oliver 动手打 Orlando.

51—52 **young**：inexperienced. **this**：fighting.

53 **villain**：①person of low birth；②serf.

56 **that says...villians**：系主语 he 的定语从句。 **begot**：was the father of.

58 **this other**：this other hand.

59 **railed on**：slandered.

60—61 **patient**：calm. **remembrance**：memory. **at accord**：at peace with each other.

66 **qualities**：accomplishments.

68—69 **exercises**：pursuits. **become**：suit.

69 **poor allottery**：small portion of the inheritance.

70—71 **go...fortunes**：自觅生计。

74 **your will**：①what you want；②what is left to you by the will.

78 **Get you**：go away.

79—80 **lost my teeth**：become old.

81 **spoke**：spoken.

OLI. Is it even so? begin you to grow upon me? I will physic your rankness, and yet give no thousand crowns neither. Holla, Dennis!

Enter DENNIS.

DEN. Calls your worship?

OLI. Was not Charles, the duke's wrestler here to speak with me?

DEN. So please you, he is here at the door, and importunes access to you.

OLI. Call him in. [*Exit* DENNIS.] 'Twill be a good way; and to-morrow the wrestling is.

Enter CHARLES.

CHA. Good morrow to your worship.

OLI. Good morrow, Monsieur Charles, what's the new news at the new court?

CHA. There's no news at the court, sir, but the old news: that is, the old duke is banished by his younger brother the new duke; and three or four loving lords have put themselves into voluntary exile with him, whose lands and revenues enrich the new duke; therefore he gives them good leave to wander.

OLI. Can you tell if Rosalind, the duke's daughter, be banished with her father?

CHA. O, no; for the duke's daughter, her cousin, so loves her, —being ever from their cradles bred together, —that she would have followed her exile, or have died to stay behind her. She is at the court, and no less beloved of her uncle than his own daughter; and never two ladies loved as they do.

OLI. Where will the old duke live?

CHA. They say he is already in the forest of Arden, and a many merry men with him; and there they live

82 Is...so：事情已到了这等地步？ **grow upon**：get the better of(凌驾……之上)。

83 physic(v.) **your rankness**：cure you of your overgrowth.

84 neither：either.伊丽莎白时代以双重否定来表示否定的用法较为普遍。

85 Calls your worship?：Does your worship call me?

88—89 So please you：if you please. **importunes...you**：begs to see you.

92 Good morrow：good morning.

97 loving lords：lords who love the old duke and are loyal to him.

99 revenues：收入。

100 good leave：full permission. **wander**：go where one likes.

103 cousin：堂妹。

105 being...together：being bred (brought up) together ever since they were in cradles.

105—106 to stay：if she were forced to stay.

106 beloved of：loved by.

110 forest of Arden：按莎士比亚所据 Thomas Lodge 中的 Rosalynde 为 Forest of the Ardennes，在法国；但莎士比亚所说的 Arden 森林则在他的故乡沃列克郡，离他母亲的家不远，是他从小熟悉的地方。

like the old Robin Hood of England. They say many young gentlemen flock to him every day, and fleet the time carelessly, as they did in the golden world.

OLI. What, you wrestle to-morrow before the new duke?

CHA. Marry, do I, sir; and I came to acquaint you with a matter. I am given, sir, secretly to understand that your younger brother Orlando hath a disposition to come in disguised against me to try a fall. To-morrow, sir, I wrestle for my credit, and he that escapes me without some broken limb shall acquit him well. Your brother is but young and tender; and, for your love, I would be loth to foil him as I must , for my own honour, if he come in: therefore, out of my love to you, I came hither to acquaint you withal, that either you might stay him from his intendment or brook such disgrace well as he shall run into, in that it is a thing of his own search and altogether against my will.

OLI. Charles, I thank thee for thy love to me, which thou shalt find I will most kindly requite. I had myself notice of my brother's purpose herein, and have by underhand means laboured to dissuade him from it, but he is resolute. I'll tell thee , Charles : it is the stubbornest young fellow of France; full of ambition, an envious emulator of every man's good parts, a secret and villanous contriver against me his natural brother: therefore use thy discretion. I had as lief thou didst break his neck as his finger. And thou wert best look to't; for if thou dost him any slight disgrace, or if he do not mightily grace himself on thee, he will practise against thee by poison, entrap thee by some treacherous device, and never leave thee till he hath ta'en thy life by some indirect means or other; for, I assure thee, —and almost with tears I speak it, —there is not one

112 **Robin Hood of England**：中世纪时英格兰有名的绿林英雄。他与同伙活动在诺丁汉附近的 Sherwood 森林，留下许多传奇故事。

113 **fleet**：pass. **carelessly**：without care，无忧无虑地。

114 **golden world**：即“黄金时代”(Golden Age)，是古希腊、罗马诗人假托的古时理想时代，人们在露天过着简单纯朴、无忧无虑的田园生活。

118 **am given...understand**：have been told in secret.

119 **disposition**：inclination，intention.

120 **fall**：bout of wrestling.

121 **for my credit**：to defend my reputation.

122 **shall...well**：will have to take good care of himself.

123 **tender**：undeveloped. **for your love**：because of the love I have for you.

123—124 **loth**：unwilling. **foil**：defeat，overthrow.

125 **hither**：here.

126 **withal**：with it. **that**：so that. **stay**：keep，stop.

126—127 **intendment**：intention. **brook**：endure，tolerate.

131 **kindly**：appropriately. **requite**：reward，repay.

131—132 **I...herein**：I myself know my brother's intention in this regard. **underhand**：indirect，secret.

135—136 **emulator**：rival. **parts**：qualities.

136—137 **contriver**：plotter.

138 **use...discretion**：do as you please. **discretion**：liberty to act at pleasure. **had as lief**：Would willingly rather.

139 **thou...to't**：you had better take care.

141 **grace...thee**：win himself honour at your expense. **practise**：plot.

144 **indirect**：underhand，secret.

so young and so villanous this day living. I speak but brotherly of him; but should I anatomize him to thee as he is, I must blush and weep and thou must look pale and wonder.

CHA. I am heartily glad I came hither to you. If he come tomorrow, I'll give him his payment: if ever he go alone again, I'll never wrestle for prize more: and so God keep your worship!

OLI. Farewell, good Charles. [Exit CHARLES.] Now will I stir this gamester. I hope I shall see an end of him; for my soul, yet I know not why, hates nothing more than he. Yet he's gentle, never schooled and yet learned, full of noble device, of all sorts enchantingly beloved, and, indeed so much in the heart of the world, and especially of my own people, who best know him, that I am altogether misprised. But it shall not be so long; this wrestler shall clear all: nothing remains but that I kindle the boy thither, which now I'll go about.

[*Exit*.

SCENE II

—*A Lawn before the* DUKE'S *Palace*.

Enter ROSALIND *and* CELIA.

CEL. I pray thee, Rosalind, sweet my coz, be merry.

ROS. Dear Celia, I show more mirth than I am mistress of, and would you yet I were merrier? Unless you could teach me to forget a banished father, you must not learn me how to remember any extraordinary pleasure.

CEL. Herein I see thou lovest me not with the full weight that I love thee. If my uncle, thy banished father, had banished thy uncle, the duke my father, so thou hadst been still with me, I could have taught my love to take thy father for mine: so wouldst thou, if

147 brotherly：with brotherly feeling.意为有碍兄弟情分，不能言尽。 **anatomize him**：describe him in detail（anatomize 原意是“解剖”、“分析”）。

151 his payment：what he deserves，即 punishment.

152—153 go alone again：leave walking unaided.意思是他一定要将 Orlando 打断骨头，使他不能行走。

152—153 more：any longer. **keep**：care for.

155 stir：provoke，instigate.

155—156 gamester：sportsman，指 Orlando. **see...him**：今后再也见不到他，即巴望他在摔跤中丧命。

158—159 device：aspiration. **of...beloved**：enchanting loved by all sorts. **all sorts**：people of all classes. **enchantingly**：in a way as being charmed.

161 misprised：despised.

162 clear all：settle everything.

163 kindle：incite. **thither**：to go there. **go about**：attend to.

I.ii

1 sweet my coz：my dear cousin.coz 为 cousin 的昵称，简缩语。

2—3 than I am mistress of：than I really possess. **you**：注意 Celia 称 Rosalind，用 thou 表示亲密；Rosalind 则因父亲被黜，自己寄人篱下，有些担心，故称 Celia，用 you 以示尊敬，此种细微之处不可忽视。

5 learn：teach.

7 Herein：in this.

9 so：provided that.

11 take：accept.

the truth of thy love to me were so righteously tempered as mine is to thee.

ROS. Well, I will forget the condition of my estate, to rejoice in yours.

CEL. You know my father hath no child but I, nor none is like to have: and, truly, when he dies, thou shalt be his heir: for what he hath taken away from thy father perforce, I will render thee again in affection; by mine honour, I will; and when I break that oath, let me turn monster. Therefore, my sweet Rose, my dear Rose, be merry.

ROS. From henceforth I will, coz, and devise sports. Let me see; what think you of falling in love?

CEL. Marry, I prithee, do, to make sport withal: but love no man in good earnest; nor no further in sport neither, than with safety of a pure blush thou mayst in honour come off again.

ROS. What shall be our sport then?

CEL. Let us sit and mock the good housewife Fortune from her wheel, that her gifts may henceforth be bestowed equally.

ROS. I would we could do so, for her benefits are mightily misplaced, and the bountiful blind woman doth most mistake in her gifts to women.

CEL. 'Tis true; for those that she makes fair she scarce makes honest, and those that she makes honest she makes very ill-favouredly.

ROS. Nay, now thou goest from Fortune's office to Nature's: Fortune reigns in gifts of the world, not in the lineaments of Nature.

Enter TOUCHSTONE

CEL. No? when Nature hath made a fair creature, may she not by Fortune fall into the fire? Though

11—12 if the truth...thee：if your love were true，being made up of such right qualities，as is my love to you. **righteously tempered**：made up of right qualities.

14 estate：state，处境。

16 but：except.

16—17 nor none is like to have：nor is he likely to have any other (children).

19 perforce：by force.

19—20 reader：return. **by mine honour**：以我的荣誉起誓。

21 Rose：Rosalind 的简缩爱称。

23 henceforth：from this time forward. **sports**：entertainments.

25 I prithee：I pray you.

25—26 to make sport withal：仅作为消遣而已。 **withal**：with it. **in good earnest**：seriously.

26—28 nor no further...off again：即使开玩笑也不宜过分，不要弄到羞涩的天真无法保护你脱身的地步。 **come off**：withdraw.此句中 no further than thou mayst come off again 意味着“不要走得太远，不能自拔”。

30—31 据希腊神话，命运女神(Fortune)手持纺车，织人类的命运，就像纺纱的妇女(housewife)，纺车起落，决定人的祸福荣辱。Celia 说如果她们能以嘲讽使其离开纺车，人类的命运就会更公平一些。 **from**：away from. **that**：so that.

33 would：wish.

34 bountiful：liberal in giving(慷慨施予的)。 **blind woman**：命运女神在施行赏罚时眼睛是遮住的，故云。

36 fair：beautiful. **scarce**：rarely.

37—38 honest：virtuous，chaste. **ill-favouredly**：ugly，favour 解义 face.

39—43 Rosalind 认为聪明美貌是造物赋予的，金钱地位才由命运安排。 **office**：power；function. **lineaments of Nature**：造物给予的容貌。 **fall into the fire**：fire 可指普通的火，也可指地狱之火。

Nature hath given us wit to flout at Fortune, hath not Fortune sent in this fool to cut off the argument?

ROS. Indeed, there is Fortune too hard for Nature, when Fortune makes Nature's natural the cutter-off of Nature's wit.

CEL. Peradventure this is not Fortune's work neither, but Nature's; who perceiving our natural wits too dull to reason of such goddesses, hath sent this natural for our whetstone: for always the dulness of the fool is the whetstone of the wits. How now, wit! whither wander you?

TOUCH. Mistress, you must come away to your father.

CEL. Were you made the messenger?

TOUCH. No, by mine honour; but I was bid to come for you.

ROS. Where learned you that oath, fool?

TOUCH. Of a certain knight that swore by his honour they were good pancakes, and swore by his honour the mustard was naught: now I'll stand to it, the pancakes were naught and the mustard was good, and yet was not the knight forsworn.

CEL. How prove you that, in the great heap of your knowledge?

ROS. Ay, marry, now unmuzzle your wisdom.

TOUCH. Stand you both forth now: stroke your chins, and swear by your beards that I am a knave.

CEL. By our beards, if we had them, thou art.

TOUCH. By my knavery, if I had it, then I were; but if you swear by that that is not, you are not forsworn: no more was this knight swearing by his honour, for he never had any; or if he had, he had sworn it away before ever he saw those pancakes or that mustard.

44 **flout**：mock.

45 **this fool**：指刚登场的 Touchstone，此弄臣名“试金石”，指其能辨别人的真伪智愚。下面又说他是“砺石”，能磨砺和激发旁人的机智。

47 **Natural**：fool；idiot.

51 **reason of**：talk sensibly about. **goddesses**：指 Fortune 与 Nature.

54 **How now，wit... you?**：Hello，clever man，where are you going? 参见谚语：“wit，whither wilt?”

58 **mine honour**：在以元音或 h 开头的名词前，my 改 mine，为诗体用法。

60 **that oath**：等于 by mine honour.

61 当时认为傻子是无 honour 可言的，只有 knights 才有荣誉，因此才引出了下面的一段话。 **Of**：from.

63 **mustard**：芥末。 **naught**：bad，worthless.

63—64 **stand to it**：swear to it.

64—65 **was not...forsworn**：had not broken his oath.

66 **heap**：amount.

68 **unmuzzle**：set free（释放；解放）。muzzle 是套在狗嘴上的皮套。

71 **thon art**：you are a knave.

73 **that that is not**：that which does not exist (their beards).

CEL. Prithee, who is't that thou meanest?

TOUCH. One that old Frederick, your father, loves.

CEL. My father's love is enough to honour him. Enough! speak no more of him; you'll be whipped for taxation one of these days.

TOUCH. The more pity, that fools may not speak wisely what wise men do foolishly.

CEL. By my troth, thou sayest true; for since the little wit that fools have was silenced, the little foolery that wise men have makes a great show. Here comes Monsieur Le Beau.

ROS. With his mouth full of news.

CEL. Which he will put on us, as pigeons feed their young.

ROS. Then we shall be news-cramm'd.

CEL. All the better; we shall be more marketable.

Enter LE BEAU

Bon jour, Monsieur Le Beau: what's the news?

LE BEAU. Fair princess, you have lost much good sport.

CEL. Sport! Of what colour?

LE BEAU. What colour, madam! How shall I answer you?

ROS. As wit and fortune will.

TOUCH. Or as the Destinies decree.

CEL. Well said: that was laid on with a trowel.

TOUCH. Nay, if I keep not my rank,—

ROS. Thou losest thy old smell.

LE BEAU. You amaze me, ladies: I would have told you of good wrestling, which you have lost the sight of.

ROS. You tell us the manner of the wrestling.

LE BEAU. I will tell you the beginning; and, if it

81—82 taxation：criticism，satire，指 Touchstone 居然说 Frederick 公爵的骑士无荣誉可言。

83 speak wisely：speak in a witty manner.这里 speak 作及物动词用，等于 talk about.

85 troth：faith.

85—86 the little wit...was silenced：这是莎士比亚批评当局钳制舆论的话，可能指 1599 年枢密院焚烧 Nashe 及 Harvey 的讽刺小册子并禁止再出版这类书的决定。

90 put on：force on.

92 news-cramm'd：filled with news.英语中有 corncrammed 一词，指先将家禽塞饱，然后再提家禽到市上去卖，可以多卖钱。下一行中 more marketable 即从此义而来。

94 *Bon jour* 〈法语〉：Good morning.

95 lost：missed.

97 colour：sort.此处很可能是文字游戏。sport 的发音与 spot 相近，法国人说英语更易混，而 spot 系指针织品图案点。

100 wit：good sense. **fortune**：mere chance.

101 Destinies：命运三女神，但也可看作整体的 Fortune，故这里动词仍用单数。

102 laid on with a trowel：说得恰到好处。 **trowel**：泥工用来涂抹灰泥的工具。 **laid on**：spread(涂灰泥)。

103 Touchstone 刚才模仿贵族口气说话，现为自己辩解。**rank**：①class；②stench.

104 old smell：Rosalind 取 rank 的第二义，与 Touchstone 打诨。

105 amaze：bewilder.

please your ladyships, you may see the end, for the best is yet to do; and here, where you are, they are coming to perform it.

CEL. Well, the beginning, that is dead and buried.

LE BEAU. There comes an old man and his three sons, —

CEL. I could match this beginning with an old tale.

LE BEAU. Three proper young men, of excellent growth and presence; —

ROS. With bills on their necks, 'Be it known unto all men by these presents.'

LE BEAU. The eldest of the three wrestled with Charles, the duke's wrestler; which Charles in a moment threw him and broke three of his ribs, that there is little hope of life in him: so he served the second, and so the third. Yonder they lie; the poor old man, their father, making such pitiful dole over them that all the beholders take his part with weeping.

ROS. Alas!

TOUCH. But what is the sport, monsieur, that the ladies have lost?

LE BEAU. Why, this that I speak of.

TOUCH. Thus men may grow wiser every day: it is the first time that ever I heard breaking of ribs was sport for ladies.

CEL. Or I, I promise thee.

ROS. But is there any else longs to feel this broken music in his sides? is there yet another dotes upon rib-breaking? Shall we see this wrestling, cousin?

LE BEAU. You must, if you stay here; for here is the place appointed for the wrestling, and they are ready to perform it.

111　to do：to come，to happen.

117—118　match... old tale：tell another story with the same beginning.指这样的开头（一个父亲和三个儿子）无非是俗套。

119—120　proper：good-looking.　**growth**：height.　**presence**：appearance.

121—122　bills：placards.　**'Be it known... '**："特此布告，俾众周知"。英语告示常以此类文字开始。　**these presents**（法律用语）：these present writings，从上文 presence 联想到 presents.

124　which Charles：the same Charles.

125　that：so that.

126　so he served the second：he treated the second (son) in the same way.

128　dole：lamentation.

129　take his part：follow suit.

137　I promise thee：I assure you (that this is also the first time for me to hear such a thing).

138　longs：前面省略了关系代词 who，第 139 行中的 dotes 同此。

138—139　broken music：①noise made by breaking ribs；②musical instrument with broken ribs or frets.

139　dotes upon：loves.

CEL. Yonder, sure, they are coming: let us now stay and see it.

Flourish. Enter DUKE FREDERICK, LORDS, ORLANDO, CHARLES, *and* ATTENDANTS.

DUKE F. Come on: since the youth will not be entreated, his own peril on his forwardness.

ROS. Is yonder the man?

LE BEAU. Even he, madam.

CEL. Alas! he is too young: yet he looks successfully.

DUKE F. How now, daughter and cousin! are you crept hither to see the wrestling?

ROS. Ay, my liege, so please you give us leave.

DUKE F. You will take little delight in it, I can tell you, there is such odds in the man: in pity of the challenger's youth, I would fain dissuade him, but he will not be entreated. Speak to him, ladies; see if you can move him.

CEL. Call him hither, good Monsieur Le Beau.

DUKE F. Do so: I'll not be by.

[DUKE *goes apart*.

LE BEAU. Monsieur the challenger, the princess calls for you.

ORL. I attend them with all respect and duty.

ROS. Young man, have you challenged Charles the wrestler?

ORL. No, fair princess; he is the general challenger: I come but in, as others do, to try with him the strength of my youth.

CEL. Young gentleman, your spirits are too bold for your years. You have seen cruel proof of this man's strength: if you saw yourself with your eyes or knew yourself with your judgment, the fear of your adventure

146 ***Flourish***：重要人物(经常是国君)出场时的喇叭声。

148—149 **entreated**：induced，这里是 dissuaded. **his own peril...forwardness**：let him take the risk for his own rashness.

150 **yonder**：that.

151 **Even**：exactly.

152—153 **successfully**：like one who is able to succeed.

154 **cousin**：泛指亲戚，虽然 Rosalind 本是他的侄女。

154 **are you crept**：have you come quietly.伊丽莎白时期运动动词常用 to be 加 p.p.的形式表完成时。

156 **my liege**：my lord. **so please you...**：if you will be kind enough to give us permission.

158 **odds**：disparity(悬殊)，此处指 superiority. **the man**：指 Charles.

170 **he is the general challenger**：he has offered to fight all comers in general.

175 **with your eyes**：clearly.

would counsel you to a more equal enterprise. We pray you, for your own sake, to embrace your own safety and give over this attempt.

ROS. Do, young sir: your reputation shall not therefore be misprised. We will make it our suit to the duke that the wrestling might not go forward.

ORL. I beseech you, punish me not with your hard thoughts, wherein I confess me much guilty, to deny so fair and excellent ladies anything. But let your fair eyes and gentle wishes go with me to my trial: wherein if I be foiled, there is but one shamed that was never gracious; if killed, but one dead that is willing to be so. I shall do my friends no wrong , for I have none to lament me; the world no injury. for in it I have nothing; only in the world I fill up a place, which may be better supplied when I have made it empty.

ROS. The little strength that I have, I would it were with you.

CEL. And mine, to eke out hers.

ROS. Fare you well. Pray heaven I be deceived in you!

CEL. Your heart's desires be with you!

CHA. Come, where is this young gallant that is so desirous to lie with his mother earth?

ORL. Ready, sir; but his will hath in it a more modest working.

DUKE F. You shall try but one fall.

CHA. No, I warrant your Grace, you shall not entreat him to a second, that have so mightily persuaded him from a first.

ORL. You mean to mock me after, you should not have mocked me before: but come your ways.

ROS. Now Hercules be thy speed, young man!

CEL. I would I were invisible, to catch the strong

177 **counsel**: advise. **a more equal enterprise**: a fight where you stand more equal chance.

178—179 **embrace**: hold on to. **give over**: give up.

180—181 **therefore**: on that account. **misprised**: undervalued. **suit**: plea.

182 **go forward**: proceed, continue.

183—184 **punish me... thoughts**: do not make me suffer by thinking badly of me.

184 **wherein**: in a matter in which. **me**: myself.

187 **foiled**: overthrown. **gracious**: graced by Fortune.

188 **one**: 指他自己。

191 **supplied**: filled.

193 **would**: wish.

195 **eke out**: add to.

196 **deceived in**: mistaken about (underestimated).

200 **to lie with his mother earth**: to return to dust, to be killed.

201—202 **his will...working**: his desire is more modest than being killed. **working**: effort, endeavour.

204 **warrant**: assure.

205 **that**: who,先行词为 you,见第 204 行。 **mightily**: vigorously. **persuaded**: tried to dissuade.

207 **You mean**: If you intend to.

208 **come your ways**: come along and begin.

209 **Hercules be thy speed**: may Hercules give you success. Hercules(或 Herakles)是希腊神话中的大力士英雄。 **speed**: success.

fellow by the leg.

[CHARLES *and* ORLANDO *wrestle*.

ROS. O excellent young man!

CEL. If I had a thunderbolt in mine eye, I can tell who should down.

[CHARLES *is thrown*. *Shout*.

DUKE F. No more, no more.

ORL. Yes, I beseech your Grace: I am not yet well breathed.

DUKE F. How dost thou, Charles?

LE BEAU. He cannot speak, my lord.

DUKE F. Bear him away. What is thy name, young man? [CHARLES *is borne out*.

ORL. Orlando, my liege; the youngest son of Sir Rowland de Boys.

DUKE F. I would thou hadst been son to some man else:
The world esteem'd thy father honourable,
But I did find him still mine enemy:
Thou shouldst have better pleas'd me with this deed,
Hadst thou descended from another house.
But fare thee well; thou art a gallant youth:
I would thou hadst told me of another father.

[*Exeunt* DUKE FREDERICK, TRAIN, *and* LE BEAU.

CEL. Were I my father, coz, would I do this?

ORL. I am more proud to be Sir Rowland's son, His youngest son; and would not change that calling, To be adopted heir to Frederick.

ROS. My father lov'd Sir Rowland as his soul, And all the world was of my father's mind:
Had I before known this young man his son.
I should have given him tears unto entreaties,
Ere he should thus have ventur'd.

215 **down** (vi.): fall;此句意为:如我目光有雷霆,我将击倒 Orlando 的对手。

218—219 **well breathed**: warmed up.

220 **How dost thou**: How do you feel.

224 **liege**: lord.

228 **esteem'd**: considered.

229 **still**: always.

231 **house**: family.

237 **calling**: name.

242 **unto**: in addition to.

CEL. Gentle cousin,
Let us go thank him and encourage him:
My father's rough and envious disposition
Sticks me at heart. Sir, you have well deserv'd:
If you do keep your promises in love
But justly, as you have exceeded all promise,
Your mistress shall be happy.

ROS. Gentleman,
[*Giving him a chain from her neck*.
Wear this for me, one out of suits with fortune,
That could give more, but that her hand lacks means.
Shall we go, coz?

CEL. Ay. Fare you well, fair gentleman.

ORL. Can I not say, I thank you? My better parts Are all thrown down, and that which here stands up Is but a quintain, a mere lifeless block.

ROS. He calls us back: my pride fell with my fortunes;
I'll ask him what he would. Did you call, sir?
Sir, you have wrestled well and overthrown
More than your enemies.

CEL. Will you go, coz?

ROS. Have with you. Fare you well.
[*Exeunt* ROSALIND *and* CELIA.

ORL. What passion hangs these weights upon my tongue?
I cannot speak to her, yet she urg'd conference.
O poor Orlando, thou art overthrown!
Or Charles or something weaker masters thee.

Re-enter LE BEAU

LE BEAU. Good sir, I do in friendship counsel you
To leave this place. Albeit you have deserv'd
High commendation, true applause and love,

246 **envious**: malicious.

247 **Sticks me at heart**: grieves my heart as if a knife were stuck there. **you have well deserv'd**: you have well deserved your victory.

249 **justly**: exactly.

253 **out of suits**: out of favour.

254 **could give**: would like to give.

257 **better parts**: intellectual qualities.

258 **thrown down**: overthrown, brought down.

259 **quintain**: dummy.骑士练习枪刺的人形靶。

266 **Have with you**: I am coming with you.

270 **urg'd conference**: invited conversation.

271 **overthrown**: 被征服。

272 **Or...or...**: Either...or.... **something weaker**: 指 Rosalind.

275 **Albeit**: Although.

Yet such is now the duke's condition
That he misconstrues all that you have done.
The duke is humorous: what he is indeed,
More suits you to conceive than I to speak of.

ORL. I thank you, sir; and pray you, tell me this;
Which of the two was daughter of the duke,
That here was at the wrestling?

LE BEAU. Neither his daughter, if we judge by manners:
But yet, indeed the smaller is his daughter:
The other is daughter to the banish'd duke,
And here detain'd by her usurping uncle,
To keep his daughter company; whose loves
Are dearer than the natural bond of sisters.
But I can tell you that of late this duke
Hath ta'en displeasure 'gainst his gentle niece,
Grounded upon no other argument
But that the people praise her for her virtues,
And pity her for her good father's sake;
And, on my life, his malice 'gainst the lady
Will suddenly break forth. Sir, fare you well:
Hereafter, in a better world than this,
I shall desire more love and knowledge of you.

ORL. I rest much bounden to you: fare you well.
[*Exit* LE BEAU.
Thus must I from the smoke into the smother;
From tyrant duke unto a tyrant brother.
But heavenly Rosalind! [*Exit*.

SCENE III

—A Room in the palace.

Enter CELIA *and* ROSALIND.

CEL. Why, cousin! why, Rosalind! Cupid have mercy! Not a word?

277 **condition**: mood, state of mind.

278 **misconstrutes**: misinterprets.

279 **humorous**: capricious(反复无常，捉摸不定)。

279—280 **what he is... speak of**: It is better for you to, imagine what he really is than for me to describe him.

283 **That here was**: who was here.

289 **whose loves**: their love for each other.伊丽莎白时代抽象名词，如 love 也可以加 s.

293 **Grounded**: based. **argument**: reason.

294 **But that**: than that.

296 **on my life**: I'll bet my life on it.

297 **fare you well**: may you fare well(祝你交好运)，也意味"再见"。

298 隐指等到真正公爵复位时再见。 **Hereafter**: At some later time.

299 I shall hope to have you as a friend and to know more about you.

300 **bounden**: indebted.

301 才穿过浓烟，又钻进烈火。 **smother**: suffocating smoke.

I.iii

1 **Cupid**: 希腊神话中的小爱神。

ROS. Not one to throw at a dog.

CEL. No, thy words are too precious to be cast away upon curs; throw some of them at me; come, lame me with reasons.

ROS. Then there were two cousins laid up; when the one should be lamed with reasons and the other mad without any.

CEL. But is all this for your father?

ROS. No, some of it is for my child's father: O, how full of briers is this working-day world!

CEL. They are but burrs, cousin, thrown upon thee in holiday foolery: if we walk not in the trodden paths, our very petticoats will catch them.

ROS. I could shake them off my coat: these burrs are in my heart.

CEL. Hem them away.

ROS. I would try, if I could cry 'hem' and have him.

CEL. Come, come; wrestle with thy affections.

ROS. O! they take the part of a better wrestler than myself!

CEL. O, a good wish upon you! you will try in time, in despite of a fall. But, turning these jests out of service, let us talk in good earnest: is it possible, on such a sudden, you should fall into so strong a liking with old Sir Rowland's youngest son?

ROS. The duke my father loved his father dearly.

CEL. Doth it therefore ensue that you should love his son dearly? By this kind of chase, I should hate him, for my father hated his father dearly; yet I hate not Orlando.

ROS. No, faith, hate him not, for my sake.

CEL. Why should I not? doth he not deserve well?

ROS. Let me love him for that; and do you love

5—6 lame me with reasons：make me lame by throwing your reasons (for your silence) at me.

7 were：would be. **laid up**：injured，incapacitated.

12 briers：thorny bushes(荆棘)，difficulties. **working-day**：everyday.

13—16 它们不过是为了取笑而扔在你身上的刺果。要是我们行路不循常规，我们的裙子就要被它们抓住。burrs 是带刺的果壳，会粘在衣裙上，古时逢节日人们每以掷这种刺果为嬉(holiday foolery). **walk not path**：越出常规。Celia 与 Rosalind 均为公主，与一摔跤手搭话，是一种越轨行为。

18 Hem them away：Clear them away by coughing.(bur 有二义：①牛蒡等带刺的草种子；②喉咙发痒。)

19—20 cry...him：如果咳一声，就能把他(Orlando)给咳出来。Rosalind 以 hem 与 him 音似所说的俏皮话。

22 take the part：are on the side.

24—25 a good wish upon you：bless you. **try**：exert your efforts (to wrestle with your affections). **in despite of a fall**：even though you risk falling.

25 turning...out of service：dismissing，setting aside.

31 chase：course of argument.

32 dearly：intensely.

34 faith：by my faith.

35 deserve well：有两义：① well deserve to be hated(值得恨)；②deserve to be well treated(值得垂青)。Celia 用的是第一义，接下去用的是第二义。

him, because I do. Look, here comes the duke.

CEL. With his eyes full of anger.

Enter DUKE FREDERICK, *with* Lords

DUKE F. Mistress, dispatch you with your safest haste,
And get you from our court.
ROS. Me, uncle?
DUKE F. You, cousin:
Within these ten days if that thou be'st found
So near our public court as twenty miles,
Thou diest for it.
ROS. I do beseech your Grace,
Let me the knowledge of my fault bear with me.
If with myself I hold intelligence,
Or have acquaintance with mine own desires,
If that I do not dream or be not frantic,—
As I do trust I am not,—then, dear uncle,
Never so much as in a thought unborn
Did I offend your highness.
DUKE F. Thus do all traitors:
If their purgation did consist in words,
They are as innocent as grace itself:
Let it suffice thee that I trust thee not.

ROS. Yet your mistrust cannot make me a traitor: Tell me whereon the likelihood depends.

DUKE F. Thou art thy father's daughter; there's enough.

ROS. So was I when your highness took his dukedom;
So was I when your highness banish'd him.
Treason is not inherited, my lord;
Or, if we did derive it from our friends,
What's that to me? my father was no traitor:

39—40 **dispatch**：hurry. **safest haste**：snch haste as will save your life，utmost speed.

43 **cousin**：kinswoman.

48 Let me bear (take) with me the knowledge of my fault.

49 要是我还有自知之明。 **intelligence**：communication，intercourse.

51 **If that**：If. **frantic**：mad.

52 **I am not**：I am not frantic.

55 **Thus do all traitors**：All traitors talk like that.如果言词就能证明他们清白。

56 **purgation**：clearance from guilt. **consist in**：depend on.

57 **grace**：God's mercy.

58 **suffice thee**：be sufficient for you to know.

60 **whereon**：on what grounds. **likelihood**：supposition (that I am a traitor).

67 **derive**：receive，inherit. **friends**：relatives.

Then, good my liege, mistake me not so much
To think my poverty is treacherous.

CEL. Dear sovereign, hear me speak.

DUKE F. Ay, Celia; we stay'd her for your sake; Else had she with her father rang'd along.

CEL. I did not then entreat to have her stay:
It was your pleasure and your own remorse.
I was too young that time to value her;
But now I know her: if she be a traitor,
Why so am I; we still have slept together,
Rose at an instant, learn'd, play'd, eat together;
And whereso'er we went, like Juno's swans,
Still we went coupled and inseparable.

DUKE F. She is too subtle for thee; and her smoothness,
Her very silence and her patience,
Speak to the people, and they pity her.
Thou art a fool: she robs thee of thy name;
And thou wilt show more bright and seem more virtuous
When she is gone. Then open not thy lips:
Firm and irrevocable is my doom
Which I have pass'd upon her; she is banish'd.

CEL. Pronounce that sentence then, on me, my liege:
I cannot live out of her company.

DUKE F. You are a fool. You, niece, provide yourself:
If you outstay the time, upon mine honour,
And in the greatness of my word, you die.

[*Exeunt* DUKE FREDERICK *and* Lords.

CEL. O my poor Rosalind! whither wilt thou go?
Wilt thou change fathers? I will give thee mine.
I charge thee, be not thou more griev'd than I am.

70 **my poverty is treacherous**: that because I am poor I am treacherous.

72 **stay'd**: kept.

73 Otherwise she would have gone wandering with her father. **rang'd**: roamed, wandered.

75 **remorse**: pity, compassion.

78 **still**: always.

79 **at an instant**: at the same moment.

80 **Juno**: 在罗马神话中,Juno 是众神之主 Jupiter 的妻子。

81 **coupled**: in pair.

82 **subtle**: cunning, deceiving.

86 **name**: reputation.

90 **doom**: judgement, sentence.

95 **provide**: prepare, equip.

98 **greatness**: power.

100 **change**: exchange.

101 **charge**: order.

ROS. I have more cause.

CEL. Thou hast not, cousin;
Prithee, be cheerful; know'st thou not, the duke
Hath banish'd me, his daughter?

ROS. That he hath not.

CEL. No, hath not? Rosalind lacks then the love Which teacheth thee that thou and I am one: Shall we be sunder'd? shall we part, sweet girl?
No: let my father seek another heir.
Therefore devise with me how we may fly,
Whither to go, and what to bear with us:
And do not seek to take your change upon you,
To bear your griefs yourself and leave me out;
For, by this heaven, now at our sorrows pale,
Say what thou canst, I'll go along with thee.

ROS. Why, whither shall we go?

CEL. To seek my uncle in the forest of Arden.

ROS. Alas, what danger will it be to us,
Maids as we are, to travel forth so far!
Beauty provoketh thieves sooner than gold.

CEL. I'll put myself in poor and mean attire,
And with a kind of umber smirch my face;
The like do you: so shall we pass along
And never stir assailants.

ROS. Were it not better,
Because that I am more than common tall,
That I did suit me all points like a man?
A gallant curtle-axe upon my thigh,
A boar-spear in my hand; and,—in my heart
Lie there what hidden woman's fear there will,—
We'll have a swashing and a martial outside,
As many other mannish cowards have
That do outface it with their semblances.

CEL. What shall I call thee when thou art a man?

104 **Prithee**：I pray you.

108—109 **sunder'd**：separated.

111 **devise**：plan，make a plan. **fly**：run away.

112 **bear**：carry.

113 **take your change upon you**：take responsibillity for your change of fortune.

115 **heaven...pale**：因为同情我们的忧愁而变得惨白的天空。

121 美貌比金钱更容易引起盗心。 **provoketh**：arouses.

122 **mean attire**：humble clothes.

123 **umber**：brown pigment（指用作颜料的棕色土）。 **smirch**：darken，sully.

124 **The like do you**：You do the same.

125 **stir**：provoke.

126—128 从 Were it...起的句子用现代英语表达是：Would it not be better，since I am unusually tall，if I should dress myself in every respect like a man?

129 **curtle-axe**：一种佩剑。

131 let whatever may be woman's hidden fear lie there.

132 **swashing**：swaggering. **outside**：appearance.

133 **mannish cowards**：cowardly men. **have**：宾语为上一行 have 的宾语。

134 **outface it**：brazen it out. **it**：代替第 131 行中的 fear. **semblances**：appearances (or bravery).

ROS. I' ll have no worse a name than Jove' s own page,
And therefore look you call me Ganymede.
But what will you be call'd?

CEL. Something that hath a reference to my state: No longer Celia, but Aliena.

ROS. But, cousin, what if we assay'd to steal
The clownish fool out of your father's court?
Would he not be a comfort to our travel?

CEL. He'll go along o'er the wide world with me;
Leave me alone to woo him. Let's away,
And get our jewels and our wealth together,
Devise the fittest time and safest way
To hide us from pursuit that will be made
After my flight. Now go we in content
To liberty and not to banishment. [*Exeunt*.

136—137 Jove's own page：Jove 即 Jupiter，他有一侍童名叫 Ganymede，专门在宴会上倒酒。

140 a reference to my state：与我的处境有关。

141 Aliena：暗示 alienated(异化)之义。

142 assay'd：attempted.

146 woo：persuade. **Let's away**：Let us go now.

150 content：contentment.

ACT II

SCENE I

—The Forest of Arden.

Enter DUKE *Senior*, AMIENS, *and other* Lords, *like Foresters.*

DUKE S. Now, my co-mates and brothers in exile,
Hath not old custom made this life more sweet
Than that of painted pomp? Are not these woods
More free from peril than the envious court?
Here feel we but the penalty of Adam,
The seasons' difference; as, the icy fang
And churlish chiding of the winter's wind,
Which, when it bites and blows upon my body,
Even till I shrink with cold, I smile and say
'This is no flattery: these are counsellors
That feelingly persuade me what I am.'
Sweet are the uses of adversity,
Which like the toad, ugly and venomous,
Wears yet a precious jewel in his head;
And this our life exempt from public haunt,
Finds tongues in trees, books in the running brooks,
Sermons in stones, and good in every thing.
I would not change it.

AMI. Happy is your Grace,
That can translate the stubbornness of fortune
Into so quiet and so sweet a style.

DUKE S. Come, shall we go and kill us venison? And yet
it irks me, the poor dappled fools,
Being native burghers of this desert city,
Should in their own confines with forked heads

II.i

DUKE Senior：the older duke.剧中始终这样称 Frederick 公爵的兄长。Duke Senior 被弟篡夺王位后流放到阿登森林。

1 co-mates：companions.

2 old custom：long familiarity.

3 painted pomp：artificial splendour.

5 but：only,no more than. **penalty of Adam**：据圣经,Adam 原住在四季常青的伊甸园(Garden of Eden),后因忤逆上帝被逐出,对他的惩罚包括受季节变更之苦,即下行中的 seasons' difference(作同位语)。

6 as：such as. **icy fang**：cold bite.

7 churlish chiding：rough roar.

8 Which：at which,承接第 9 行中的动词 smile.

11 feelingly：through my senses. **persuade me**：make me know.

12 逆运也有其好处。 **uses**：benefits. **adversity**：bad fortune.

14 precious jewel：伊丽莎白时代传说癞蛤蟆本身有毒,而其头顶上有一颗珍贵的宝石叫蟾蜍石(toadstone),能解百毒。

15 exempt：cut off. **public haunt**：society of men.

18 your Grace：殿下。对公爵的尊称。

19—20 translate：transform. **style**：style of living.

21 us：for ourselves. **venison**：wild animal hunted for food.

22 irks：distresses. **dappled**：spotted(有花斑的)。 **fools**：innocents,simple creatures.

23 burghers：citizens. **desert city**：指阿登森林。

24 confines：territories. **forked heads**：打猎用的叉状箭头。

Have their round haunches gor'd.
First Lord. Indeed, my lord,
The melancholy Jaques grieves at that;
And, in that kind, swears you do more usurp
Than doth your brother that hath banish'd you.
To-day my Lord of Amiens and myself
Did steal behind him as he lay along
Under an oak whose antique root peeps out
Upon the brook that brawls along this wood;
To the which place a poor sequester'd stag,
That from the hunters' aim had ta'en a hurt,
Did come to languish; and, indeed, my lord,
The wretched animal heav'd forth such groans
That their discharge did stretch his leathern coat
Almost to bursting, and the big round tears
Cours'd one another down his innocent nose
In piteous chase; and thus the hairy fool,
Much marked of the melancholy Jaques,
Stood on the extremest verge of the swift brook,
Augmenting it with tears.
DUKE S. But what said Jaques?
Did he not moralize this spectacle?
First *Lord*. O, yes, into a thousand similes.
First, for his weeping into the needless stream;
'Poor deer,' quoth he, 'thou mak'st a testament
As worldlings do, giving thy sum of more
To that which had too much:' then, being there alone,
Left and abandon'd of his velvet friends;
''Tis right,' quoth he; 'thus misery doth part
The flux of company:' anon a careless herd,
Full of the pasture, jumps along by him
And never stays to greet him; 'Ay' quoth Jaques,
'Sweep on, you fat and greasy citizens;
'Tis just the fashion; wherefore do you look

25 round haunches：圆鼓鼓的腹部。 **gor'd**：wounded deeply.

28 in that kind：on that point (of hunting). **swears**：declares.

31 along：stretched out.

32 antique：ancient.

33 brawls：gurgles.

34 the which：this.在中世纪英语中 which 曾是名词。 **sequester'd**：separated (from the herd).

35 ta'en a hurt：received a wound.

38 their discharge：the discharge of the groans(发出那样的呻吟)。

40 cours'd：chased, pursued.

42 Much marked of：closely observed by.

44 Augmenting it with tears：adding tears to the water of the river.

46 moralize this spectacle：对此情抒发一通议论。

47 similes：comparisons.

48 for：about, concerning. **needless**：not needing more water.

50 worldings：humans(世人)。 **sum of more**：additional amount.

51 that which：those who. **then**：承接第 48 行中的 First. **being there**：前面省略了 for.

52 of：by. **velvet friends**：soft-coated family.

53 part：turn away.

54 flux：continuous stream. **company**：fellowship. **anon**：presently. **careless**：carefree.

55 Full of the pasture：well-fed with grass.

56 stays：stops.

57 Sweep：pass. **greasy**：oily, rich.

Upon that poor and broken bankrupt there?'
Thus most invectively he pierceth through
The body of the country, city, court,
Yea, and of this our life; swearing that we
Are mere usurpers, tyrants, and what's worse,
To fright the animals and to kill them up
In their assign'd and native dwelling-place.

DUKE S. And did you leave him in this contemplation?

SEC. LORD. We did, my lord, weeping and commenting
Upon the sobbing deer.

DUKE S. Show me the place.
I love to cope him in these sullen fits,
For then he's full of matter.

SEC. LORD. I'll bring you to him straight.

[*Exeunt*.

SCENE II

—A Room in the Palace.

Enter DUKE FREDERICK, Lords, *and* Attendants.

DUKE F. Can it be possible that no man saw them?
It cannot be: some villains of my court
Are of consent and sufferance in this.

FIRST LORD. I cannot hear of any that did see her.
The ladies, her attendants of her chamber,
Saw her a-bed; and, in the morning early
They found the bed untreasur'd of their mistress.

SEC. LORD. My lord, the roynish clown, at whom so oft
Your Grace was wont to laugh, is also missing.
Hisperia, the princess' gentlewoman,
Confesses that she secretly o'erheard
Your daughter and her cousin much commend

59 broken: ruined. **bankrupt**: destitute creature.

60 invectively: with violent censure. **pierceth through**: attacks (as with arrows).

61 body: collective.

63 mere: sheer. **what's worse**: things that are still worse.

64 kill them up: kill them all off.

65 assign'd: appointed (by God).

72 cope: meet. **sullen fits**: melancholy moods.

73 matter: good sense.

II.ii

3 of consent and sufferance in this: in consent and connivance with this (escape) and have allowed it (知情串通)。

4 hear of: learn of, find out.

6 Saw her a-bed: put her to bed.

7 untreasur'd: robbed of the treasure.

8 roynish: 下贱的。

10 wont: accustomed.

The parts and graces of the wrestler
That did but lately foil the sinewy Charles;
And she believes, wherever they are gone,
That youth is surely in their company.

DUKE F. Send to his brother; fetch that gallant hither;
If he be absent, bring his brother to me;
I'll make him find him. Do this suddenly,
And let not search and inquisition quail
To bring again these foolish runaways.

[*Exeunt*.

SCENE III

—*Before* OLIVER'S *House*.

Enter ORLANDO *and* ADAM, *meeting*.

ORL. Who's there?

ADAM. What! my young master? O my gentle master!
O my sweet master! O you memory
Of old Sir Rowland! why, what make you here?
Why are you virtuous? why do people love you?
And wherefore are you gentle, strong, and valiant?
Why would you be so fond to overcome
The bonny prizer of the humorous duke?
Your praise is come too swiftly home before you.
Know you not, master, to some kind of men
Their graces serve them but as enemies?
No more do yours: your virtues, gentle master,
Are sanctified and holy traitors to you.
O, what a world is this, when what is comely
Envenoms him that bears it!

ORL. Why, what's the matter?

ADAM. O unhappy youth!
Come not within these doors; within this roof

14 **parts and graces**：qualities and elegant manners.

18 **Send to**：send somebody to. **gallant**：fine gentleman.

21 **suddenly**：at once.

22 **inquisition**：inquiry. **quail**：slacken(放松)。

23 不定式短语作名词 search and inquisition 的定语。 **bring again**：brinag back.

II.iii

3 **memory**：reminder.

4 **what make you**：what are you doing.

6 **wherefor**：why.

7 **fond**：foolish. **to**：as to.

8 **bonny prizer**：stout prize-fighter. **humorous**：capricious.

9 **is come**：has come,旧时行动动词完成式。

10—11 **to some...enemies**：There are certain people whose good qualities only do them harm.

12 **No more do**：so do. **yours**：your graces.

13 美德本来是圣洁的,Orlando 却因美德而招祸,美德成了他的叛徒(traitors),像 sanctified and holy traitors 那样,把互相矛盾的概念排列在一起,修辞上称为 Oxymoron(矛盾修饰法)。

14 **comely**：graceful.

15 **Envenoms**：poisons.

18 **within this roof**：in this house.

The enemy of all your graces lives.
Your brother,—no, no brother; yet the son,—
Yet not the son, I will not call him son
Of him I was about to call his father,—
Hath heard your praises, and this night he means
To burn the lodging where you use to lie,
And you within it: if he fail of that,
He will have other means to cut you off.
I overheard him and his practices.
This is no place; this house is but a butchery:
Abhor it, fear it, do not enter it.

ORL. Why, whither, Adam, wouldst thou have me go?

ADAM. No matter whither, so you come not here.

ORL. What! wouldst thou have me go and beg my food?
Or with a base and boisterous sword enforce
A thievish living on the common road?
This I must do, or know not what to do:
Yet this I will not do, do how I can;
I rather will subject me to the malice
Of a diverted blood and bloody brother.

ADAM. But do not so. I have five hundred crowns,
The thrifty hire I sav'd under your father,
Which I did store to be my foster-nurse
When service should in my old limbs lie lame,
And unregarded age in corners thrown.
Take that; and He that doth the ravens feed,
Yea, providently caters for the sparrow,
Be comfort to my age! Here is the gold;
All this I give you. Let me be your servant:
Though I look old, yet I am strong and lusty;
For in my youth I never did apply
Hot and rebellious liquors in my blood,

21 **him**：指 Sir Rowland.

23 **praises**：achievements to which praise is due.

24 **use to**：are accustomed to. **lie**：sleep.

26 **cut you off**：kill you.

27 **practices**：plots.

28 **place**：安身之处。 **butchery**：屠场。

32 **so**：so long as.

35 **base and boisterous**：evil and violent.

36 做断路强盗。

37 我只好这样做，否则就不知道该怎么办。

38 **do how I can**：whatever else I may have to do.

40 **a diverted blood**：a blood relationship that has turned from its natural direction. **bloody**：murderous.

41 **crowns**：旧时值五先令的货币。

42 **thrifty hire I sav'd**：the thrifty savings from my wages.

43 **foster-nurse**：养老之本。此词本义为"奶娘"。

44 When my aged limbs are lame and unfit for service.

45 **unregarded**：unnoticed.

46—47 **He...sparrow**：用食物喂乌鸦的上帝，必不会忘记把麻雀喂饱。上句语出自《圣经·旧约·约伯记》第 38 章第 41 节，下句出自《圣经·新约·马太福音》第 10 章第 29 节。 **He**：上帝。

50 **lusty**：vigorous.

52 **rebellious**：causing disorder in the body.

Nor did not with unbashful forehead woo
The means of weakness and debility;
Therefore my age is as a lusty winter,
Frosty, but kindly. let me go with you;
I'll do the service of a younger man
In all your business and necessities.

ORL. O good old man! how well in thee appears
The constant service of the antique world.
When service sweat for duty, not for meed!
Thou art not for the fashion of these times,
Where none will sweat but for promotion,
And having that, do choke their service up
Even with the having: it is not so with thee.
But, poor old man, thou prun'st a rotten tree,
That cannot so much as a blossom yield,
In lieu of all thy pains and husbandry.
But come thy ways, we'll go along together,
And ere we have thy youthful wages spent,
We'll light upon some settled low content.

ADAM. Master, go on, and I will follow thee
To the last gasp with truth and loyalty.
From seventeen years till now almost fourscore
Here lived I, but now live here no more.
At seventeen years many their fortunes seek;
But at fourscore it is too late a week:
Yet fortune cannot recompense me better
Than to die well and not my master's debtor.

[*Exeunt*.

SCENE IV

—The Forest of Arden.

Enter ROSALIND *in boy's clothes*, CELIA *dressed like a shepherdess*, *and* TOUCHSTONE.

ROS. O Jupiter, how weary are my spirits!

53 **with unbashful forehead**：shamelessly. **woo**：seek.

54 **The means of**：the things that cause.

60 **constant**：faithful. **antique**：ancient.

61 **sweat**：for "sweated"，动词语尾为 t 时，"-ed"常省略。**meed**：reward.

62 **these**：the present.

63 **but for**：except for.

64 **choke...up**：smother.

65 **Even with the having**：As soon as they get promotion.

66 **prun'st**：修枝。 **a rotten tree**：Orlando 自喻为朽木。

68 **In lieu of**：in return for. **pains**：cares. **husbandry**：cultivation.

69 **come thy ways**：come along.

70 **youthful wages**：wages earned when you were young.

71 **light upon**：find. **settled low content**：settled life with a low standard of satisfaction.

73 **truth**：faithfulness.

77 **a week**：in the day.

II.iv

1 **Jupiter**：罗马神话中众神之王。伊丽莎白时代人们常以上帝或 Jupiter 起誓，或感叹。

TOUCH. I care not for my spirits if my legs were not weary.

ROS. I could find it in my heart to disgrace my man's apparel and to cry like a woman; but I must comfort the weaker vessel, as doublet and hose ought to show itself courageous to petticoat: therefore courage, good Aliena.

CEL. I pray you, bear with me: I cannot go no further.

TOUCH. For my part, I had rather bear with you than bear you; yet I should bear no cross if I did bear you, for I think you have no money in your purse.

ROS. Well, this is the forest of Arden.

TOUCH. Ay, now am I in Arden; the more fool I: when I was at home, I was in a better place: but travellers must be content.

ROS. Ay, be so, good Touchstone. Look you, who comes here; a young man and an old in solemn talk.

Enter CORIN *and* SILVIUS.

COR. That is the way to make her scorn you still.

SIL. O Corin, that thou knew'st how I do love her!

COR. I partly guess; for I have lov'd ere now.

SIL. No, Corin; being old, thou canst not guess,
Though in thy youth thou wast as true a lover
As ever sigh'd upon a midnight pillow:
But if thy love were ever like to mine,—
As sure I think did never man love so,—
How many actions most ridiculous
Hast thou been drawn to by thy fantasy?

COR. Into a thousand that I have forgotten.

SIL. O! thou didst then ne'er love so heartily.

4—5 I could find something in my heart to disgrace my man's apparel and to make me cry like a woman. **apparel**：dress.

5—6 **comfort**：cheer up. **weaker vessel**：女人，语出《圣经·新约·彼得前书》第 3 章第 7 节。 **doublet and hose**：男人穿的紧身上衣和灯笼式短裤，此处用来指男人。修辞上称为 metonymy（转喻），下面的 petticoat（裙子）用来指女人，同一修辞手法。

9—10 **bear**：be patient. **cannot go no further**：伊丽莎白时代常用双重否定来加重否定的语气。

11—14 Touchstone 在玩弄文字游戏，首先是 bear（= shoulder v.t.）与 bear with 这一对词；接下来是 cross 一词，既可表示"负担"（基督受罚时背负的十字架），又可表示金钱（当时在硬币上打有十字）。

21 **still**：always.

22 **that**：I wish that.

25 **Though**：even though.

27 **like to**：like，similar to.

28 **sure**：really. **did never man love**：man never loved.

30 **to**：into. **fantasy**：fanciful love-thoughts（痴情）。

If thou remember'st not the slightest folly
That ever love did make thee run into,
Thou hast not lov'd:
Or if thou hast not sat as I do now,
Wearing thy hearer with thy mistress' praise,
Thou hast not lov'd:
Or if thou hast not broke from company
Abruptly, as my passion now makes me,
Thou hast not lov'd. O Phebe, Phebe, Phebe!

[*Exit*.

ROS. Alas, poor shepherd! searching of thy wound, I have by hard adventure found mine own.

TOUCH. And I mine. I remember, when I was in love I broke my sword upon a stone, and bid him take that for coming a-night to Jane Smile; and I remember the kissing of her batler and the cow's dugs that her pretty chopped hands had milked; and I remember the wooing of a peascod instead of her, from whom I took two cods, and giving her them again, said with weeping tears, 'Wear these for my sake.' We that are true lovers run into strange capers; but as all is mortal in nature, so is all nature in love mortal in folly.

ROS. Thou speakest wiser than thou art ware of.

TOUCH. Nay, I shall ne'er be ware of mine own wit till I break my shins against it.

ROS. Jove, Jove! this shepherd's passion
Is much upon my fashion.

TOUCH. And mine; but it grows something stale with me.

CEL. I pray you, one of you question yond man, If he for gold will give us any food:
I faint almost to death.

TOUCH. Holla, you clown!

37 Wearing：wearying. **with thy mistress' praise**：by praising the woman you love.

39 broke：broken.

43 searching of：probing.

44 by hard adventure：by ill chance(不幸地)。

46—47 him：①指 the stone；②指 the rival. **that**：the sword cut 要是再来会 Jane Smile，便接受如此下场。Jane Smile 是 Touchstone 情人的名字。 **a-night**：at night.

48 batler：洗衣棒。 **dugs**：乳头。

49 chopped：chapped(皲裂的)。

50 peascod：豌豆荚。相传古时乡间风俗，女方若接受并佩戴男方赠的豆荚，便表示愿意以身相许。 **whom**：which，指 peascod.

51 cods：peas. **her**：the peascod.

53 capers：fooleries.

54—55 mortal：①not living forever；② extreme. 第 54 行中第一个词 mortal 取义①，第二个取义②。 **all nature in love**：everyone in love. **mortal in folly**：extremely foolish.

56 ware：aware.

57 be ware of：beware of(留神)，此处 Touchstone 所用 ware 的另一义与 Rosalind 做文字游戏。

60 upon my fashion：after my fashion(与我的失恋相像)。

61 something：somewhat.

63 yond：yonder，over there.

64 gold：money.

66 clown：Touchstone 称呼乡下人用 clown，但同时有“小丑”之义，下一行中 Rosalind 即以此相嬉。

ROS. Peace, fool: he's not thy kinsman.

COR. Who calls?

TOUCH. Your betters, sir.

COR. Else are they very wretched.

ROS. Peace, I say. Good even to you, friend.

COR. And to you, gentle sir, and to you all.

ROS. I prithee, shepherd, if that love or gold Can in this desert place buy entertainment,
Bring us where we may rest ourselves and feed.
Here's a young maid with travel much oppress'd,
And faints for succour.

COR. Fair sir, I pity her,
And wish, for her sake more than for mine own,
My fortunes were more able to relieve her;
But I am shepherd to another man,
And do not shear the fleeces that I graze:
My master is of churlish disposition
And little recks to find the way to heaven
By doing deeds of hospitality.
Besides, his cote, his flocks, and bounds of feed
Are now on sale; and at our sheepcote now,
By reason of his absence, there is nothing
That you will feed on; but what is, come see,
And in my voice most welcome shall you be.

ROS. What is he that shall buy his flock and pasture?

COR. That young swain that you saw here but erewhile,
That little cares for buying anything.

ROS. I pray thee, if it stand with honesty,
Buy thou the cottage, pasture, and the flock,
And thou shalt have to pay for it of us.

CEL. And we will mend thy wages. I like this place,
And willingly could waste my time in it.

70 **Else**：Otherwise.

71 **even**：evening.

73 **if that**：if.

74 **entertainment**：hospitality，food and shelter.

75 **feed**：宾语仍为 ourselves，省略。

76 **oppress'd**：tired out.

77 **for succour**：in quest of help.

81—82 羊儿归我饲养，羊毛却不归我剪。

83 **churlish**：miserly.

84 **recks**：cares.

86 **cote**：cottage. **bounds of feed**：pasture-land.

87 **sheepcote**：cottage for a keeper of sheep.

89 **what is**：what there is，是 come see (come to see)的宾语。

90 **in my voice**：as far as I can say.

91 **What**：what person.

94 **erewhile**：a short time ago.

96 **stand with**：be consistent with.

98 And you will have the money to pay for it from us.

99 **mend**：increase.

100 **waste**：spend.

COR. Assuredly the thing is to be sold:
Go with me: if you like upon report
The soil, the profit, and this kind of life,
I will your very faithful feeder be,
And buy it with your gold right suddenly.

[*Exeunt*.

SCENE V

—Another Part of the Forest.

Enter AMIENS, JAQUES, *and Others*.

SONG

AMI. Under the greenwood tree
Who loves to lie with me,
And turn his merry note
Unto the sweet bird's throat.
Come hither, come hither, come hither:
Here shall he see
No enemy
But winter and rough weather.

JAQ. More, more, I prithee, more.

AMI. It will make you melancholy, Monsieur Jaques.

JAQ. I thank it. More! I prithee, more. I can suck melancholy out of a song as a weasel sucks eggs. More! I prithee, more.

AMI. My voice is ragged; I know I cannot please you.

JAQ. I do not desire you to please me; I do desire you to sing. Come, more; another stanzo: call you them stanzos?

AMI. What you will, Monsieur Jaques.

102 **upon report**：after getting a full report.

104 **feeder**：servant.

105 **right suddenly**：at once.

II.v

2 **Who**：Anyone who. **lie**：sleep, spend the night.

3 **turn**：adapt. **note**：tune.

4 **unto**：to. **throat**：歌喉，转喻为歌。

8 **But**：except.

13 **weasel**：鼬鼠。

15 **ragged**：hoarse.

18 **stanzo**〈意大利语〉：stanza，诗节，当时为新的外来语。

JAQ. Nay, I care not for their names; they owe me nothing. Will you sing?

AMI. More at your request than to please myself.

JAQ. Well then, if ever I thank any man, I'll thank you: but that they call compliment is like the encounter of two dog-apes, and when a man thanks me heartily, methinks I have given him a penny and he renders me the beggarly thanks. Come, sing; and you that will not, hold your tongues.

AMI. Well, I'll end the song. Sirs, cover the while; the duke will drink under this tree. He hath been all this day to look you.

JAQ. And I have been all this day to avoid him. He is too disputable for my company: I think of as many matters as he, but I give heaven thanks, and make no boast of them. Come, warble; come.

SONG.

AMI. Who doth ambition shun, [*All together here*.
And loves to live i' the sun,
Seeking the food he eats,
And pleas'd with what he gets.
Come hither, come hither, come hither:
Here shall he see
No enemy
But winter and rough weather.

JAQ. I'll give you a verse to this note, that I made yesterday in despite of my invention.

AMI. And I'll sing it.

JAQ. Thus it goes:

If it do come to pass
That any man turn ass,

21—22 they. . . nothing：Jaques 开玩笑说他只对欠他债的人的名字感兴趣。

26 dog-apes：baboons（狒狒）。

28 you：Jaques 对在场的其他人说话。

30 cover：lay the table. **the while**：in the meanwhile.

32 to look you：looking for you.

34 disputable：fond of argument.其实 Jaques 本人才真正喜欢争论。

36 warble：sing as a bird does.

39 live. . . sun：live a free,open-air life.

46 note：tune.

47 in despite of my invention："(just) to punish my imagination" (for trying to write poetry：Jaques thinks poets are foolish).

50 come to pass：happen.

51 turn ass：become a fool.

Leaving his wealth and ease.
A stubborn will to please,
Ducdame, ducdame, ducdame:
Here shall he see
Gross fools as he,
An if he will come to me.

AMI. What's that '*ducdame?*'

JAQ. 'Tis a Greek invocation to call fools into a circle. I'll go sleep if I can; if I cannot, I'll rail against all the first-born of Egypt.

AMI. And I'll go seek the duke: his banquet is prepared. [*Exeunt severally*.

SCENE VI

—Another Part of the Forest.

Enter ORLANDO *and* ADAM.

ADAM. Dear master, I can go no further. O! I die for food. Here lie I down, and measure out my grave. Farewell, kind master.

ORL. Why, how now, Adam! no greater heart in thee? Live a little; comfort a little; cheer thyself a little. If this uncouth forest yield anything savage, I will either be food for it, or bring it for food to thee. Thy conceit is nearer death than thy powers. For my sake be comfortable, hold death awhile at the arm's end, I will here be with thee presently, and if I bring thee not something to eat, I will give thee leave to die: but if thou diest before I come, thou art a mocker of my labour. Well said! thou lookest cheerly, and I'll be with thee quickly. Yet thou liest in the bleak air: come, I will bear thee to some shelter, and thou shalt not die for lack of a dinner, if there live anything in this desert. Cheerly, good Adam. [*Exeunt*.

54 Ducdame：三音节词。历来对此词无确解，一般认为此词是 Jaques 杜撰的。

57 An if：if.

61 the first-born of Egypt：据《圣经·旧约·出埃及记》第 12 章，上帝为惩罚埃及虐待犹太人，将埃及所有家庭的长子杀害。

62 banquet：a light meal(点心)。

II.vi

2 die for：be dying for want of. **measure out**：mark out by lying down.

4 heart：courage.

5 live a little：live a little longer. **comfort**：take heart.

6 uncouth：wild. **anything savage**：any wild animal.

8 conceit：imagination.

8—9 powers：strength. **comfortable**：cheerful.

11 leave：permission.

12—13 mocker of my labour：不领我的情。 **well said**：well done.此时 Adam 略微笑了一下。 **cheerly**：cheerful.

SCENE VII

—Another Part of the Forest.

A table set out. Enter DUKE *Senior*, AMIENS Lords *like Outlaws.*

DUKE S. I think he be transform'd into a beast, For I can nowhere find him like a man.

First Lord. My lord, he is but even now gone hence:
Here was he merry, hearing of a song.

DUKE S. If he, compact of bars grow musical, We shall have shortly discord in the spheres. Go, seek him: tell him I would speak with him.

FIRST LORD. He saves my labour by his own approach.

Enter JAQUES.

DUKE S. Why, how now, monsieur! what a life is this,
That your poor friends must woo your company?
What, you look merrily!

JAQ. A fool, a fool! I met a fool i' the forest,
A motley fool; a miserable world!
As I do live by food, I met a fool;
Who laid him down and bask'd him in the sun,
And rail'd on Lady Fortune in good terms,
In good set terms, and yet a motley fool.
'Good morrow, fool,' quoth I. 'No, sir,' quoth he,
'Call me not fool till heaven hath sent me fortune.'
And then he drew a dial from his poke,
And, looking on it with lack-lustre eye,
Says very wisely, 'It is ten o'clock;
Thus may we see,' quoth he, 'how the world wags:
'Tis but an hour ago since it was nine,

II.vii

2 **like**：in the shape of.

3 **even now**：just.

6 **compact of**：made up of. **bars**：discords.

7 **spheres**：heavens.当时一般信奉古希腊天文学家 Ptolemy(托勒密)的学说，认为所有行星绕地球运行，并产生和谐悦耳的天籁。

8 **would**：wish to.

3 **woo**：seek to gain.

6 **motley fool**：穿新衣的傻子。西方宫廷小丑都身穿几种颜色的布拼成的衣服。

9,10 **terms**：expressions.

10 **good set terms**：elegant formal rhetoric，经典的修辞法是一套洋八股。

12 英语中有"Fortune favours fools"("愚人多福")的成语。

13 **dial**：一说是可携带的 sundial(日晷)；另一说是 pocket watch(怀表)。英国 1540 年开始制作怀表，起初仅一枚指针，用以计小时。 **poke**：pocket.

16 **wags**：goes on its way.

And after one hour more 'twill be eleven;
And so, from hour to hour we ripe and ripe,
And then from hour to hour we rot and rot,
And thereby hangs a tale.' When I did hear
The motley fool thus moral on the time,
My lungs began to crow like chanticleer,
That fools should be so deep-contemplative,
And I did laugh sans intermission
An hour by his dial. O noble fool!
A worthy fool! Motley's the only wear.

DUKE S. What fool is this?

JAQ. O worthy fool! One that hath been a courtier,
And says, if ladies be but young and fair,
They have the gift to know it; and in his brain, —
Which is as dry as the remainder biscuit
After a voyage, —he hath strange places cramm'd
With observation, the which he vents
In mangled forms. O that I were a fool!
I am ambitious for a motley coat.

DUKE S. Thou shalt have one.

JAQ. It is my only suit;
Provided that you weed your better judgments
Of all opinion that grows rank in them
That I am wise. I must have liberty
Withal, as large a charter as the wind,
To blow on whom I please; for so fools have:
And they that are most galled with my folly,
They most must laugh. And why, sir, must they so?
The 'why' is plain as way to parish church:
He that a fool doth very wisely hit
Doth very foolishly, although he smart,
Not to seem senseless of the bob; if not,
The wise man's folly is anatomiz'd

21 **thereby...tale**：there is a moral lesson to be drawn from that.

22 **moral**：moralize.

23 **chanticleer**：cock，源自法国的《列那狐的故事》。

25 **sans**〈法语〉：without. **intermission**：pause.

27 **only wear**：only proper dress to wear.意为只有傻子才真正值得称道。

35 **vents**：gives forth.

36 **mangled**：confused. **that I were a fool**：how I wish I were a fool.

37 **ambitious for**：strongly desirous of.

39 **suit**：双关语①petition；②dress.

40 **weed**：①拔杂草，引申为②rid.

43 **Withal**：as well. **as large a charter**：as broad a license.

44 **so**：this liberty.

45 **galled with**：hurt by.

46 **why**：reason.

47 **as...church**：像去教堂的路上一样（清楚）。

49 **Doth very foolishly**：is very foolish. **smart**：feels hurt.

50 **bob**：taunt. **if not**：if he does not seem senseless...

51 **anatomiz'd**：dissected，exposed.

Even by the squandering glances of the fool.
Invest me in my motley; give me leave
To speak my mind, and I will through and through
Cleanse the foul body of th' infected world,
If they will patiently receive my medicine.

DUKE S. Fie on thee! I can tell what thou wouldst do.

JAQ. What, for a counter, would I do, but good?

DUKE S. Most mischievous foul sin, in chiding sin:
For thou thyself hast been a libertine,
As sensual as the brutish sting itself;
And all the embossed sores and headed evils,
That thou with licence of free foot hast caught,
Wouldst thou disgorge into the general world.

JAQ. Why, who cries out on pride,
That can therein tax any private party?
Doth it not flow as hugely as the sea,
Till that the weary very means do ebb?
What woman in the city do I name,
When that I say the city-woman bears
The cost of princes on unworthy shoulders?
Who can come in and say that I mean her,
When such a one as she such is her neighbour?
Or what is he of basest function,
That says his bravery is not of my cost, —
Thinking that I mean him, —but therein suits
His folly to the mettle of my speech?

52 **squandering**：random. **glances**：satirical hits.

53 **Invest**：Dress. **leave**：permission.

55 **infected**：diseased.

56 **patiently**：①passively;②like a sick person.

57 **Fie on thee**：don't be silly.

59 **for a counter**：to wage,a worthless taken. **but**：except.

60 这一行的主语和谓语是 You will do...,已省略。 **mischievous**：wicked.

62 **libertine**：one who leads a licentious life.

63 **brutish sting**：animal lust (sexual desire).

64—66 句子倒装。语序应为 thou would disgorge all the...into.

64 **embossed**：swollen. **headed**：as boils come to a "head",指杨梅疮。

65 **licence of free foot**：licentious living.

66 **disgorge**：pour out. **general world**：world in general.

67—84 Jaques 宣称他攻击的是某一种类型的人,而不是任何个人。谁要是应声而起,便说明他该在被攻击之列。莎士比亚时代的作家和批评家经常以此来回答指责他们作人身攻击的人。

67 **cries out on**：denounces. **pride**：ostentation. extravagance.

68 **tax**：accuse. **private party**：particular individual.

69 **it**：指 pride. **flow as hugely as the sea**：如沧海横流。

70 **Till that**：till. **weary**：exhausted. **very means**：basic sources. **ebb**：run dry.

72 **When that**：when. **city-woman**：citizen's wife.

73 **the cost of princes**：clothes so costly that only princes could afford them.

74 **Who**：which city-woman.

75 when her neighbour is just like herself.

76 **what is he of basest function**：is there any man in the lowest employment.

77 **bravery**：fine clothing. **not of my cost**：not paid for by me (implying that I should mind my own business).

78—79 **suits...speech**：in saying this his folly fits the substance (mettle,metal) of what I have talked about. **mettle**：substance.

There then; how then? what then? Let me see wherein
My tongue hath wrong'd him: if it do him right,
Then he hath wrong'd himself; if he be free,
Why then, my taxing like a wild goose flies,
Unclaim'd of any man. But who comes here?

Enter ORLANDO, *with his sword drawn*.

ORL. Forbear, and eat no more.

JAQ. Why, I have eat none yet.

ORL. Nor shalt not, till necessity be serv'd.

JAQ. Of what kind should this cock come of?

DUKE S. Art thou thus bolden'd, man, by thy distress, Or else a rude despiser of good manners, That in civility thou seem'st so empty?

ORL. You touch'd my vein at first: the thorny point
Of bare distress hath ta'en from me the show
Of smooth civility: yet I am inland bred
And know some nurture. But forbear, I say:
He dies that touches any of this fruit
Till I and my affairs are answered.

JAQ. An you will not be answered with reason, I must die.

DUKE S. What would you have? Your gentleness shall force
More than your force move us to gentleness.

ORL. I almost die for food; and let me have it.

DUKE S. Sit down and feed, and welcome to our table.

ORL. Speak you so gently? Pardon me, I pray you:
I thought that all things had been savage here,
And therefore put I on the countenance
Of stern commandment. But whate'er you are

80 There then: There is my opinion. **how then? what then?**: What can you argue against it?

81 do him right: describe him correctly.

82 he hath wrong'd himself: put himself in the wrong. **free**: innocent (of my charge).

83 taxing: criticism.

1 Forbear: Stand back. **eat**: have eaten.

3 Nor shalt not: Nor shall you eat any. **necessity**: those in real need.

4 kind: family, ancestral stock. **cock**: rude fellow.

5 bolden'd: emboldened.

6—7 that: so that. **civility**: good manners. **empty**: lacking.

8 touch'd my vein: 当时的医生常用放血的方法来治病，此语意为"一下子就找到血管"，喻"一针见血"或"一言道破"。 **at first**: in your first question. **thorny point**: difficult plight.

11 inland bred: brought up in the city.

12 know some nurture: have had some education or training.

13 fruit: dessert.

14 answered: attended to.

15 An: if. Jaques 讲此句时，开始吃东西。

17—19 Your...gentleness: 第一个 force 是动词，第二个 force 是名词，move 前省略了 shall.

23 gently: like a gentleman.

26 countenance: face.

27 commandment: command.

That in this desert inaccessible,
Under the shade of melancholy boughs,
Lose and neglect the creeping hours of time;
If ever you have look'd on better days,
If ever been where bells have knoll'd to church,
If ever sat at any good man's feast,
If ever from your eyelids wip'd a tear,
And know what 'tis to pity, and be pitied,
Let gentleness my strong enforcement be:
In the which hope I blush, and hide my sword.

DUKE S. True is it that we have seen better days,
And have with holy bell been knoll'd to church,
And sat at good men's feasts, and wip'd our eyes
Of drops that sacred pity hath engender'd;
And therefore sit you down in gentleness
And take upon command what help we have
That to your wanting may be minister'd.

ORL. Then but forbear your food a little while,
Whiles, like a doe, I go to find my fawn
And give it food. There is an old poor man,
Who after me hath many a weary step
Limp'd in pure love: till he be first suffic'd,
Oppress'd with two weak evils, age and hunger,
I will not touch a bit.

DUKE S. Go find him out,
And we will nothing waste till you return.

ORL. I thank ye; and be bless'd for your good comfort! [*Exit*.

DUKE S. Thou seest we are not all alone unhappy:
This wide and universal theatre
Presents more woful pageants than the scene
Wherein we play in.

JAQ. All the world's a stage,
And all the men and women merely players:

28 **desert inaccessible**：remote and uninhabited place.

30 **Lose and neglect**：waste and take no notice of.

31 **look'd on**：seen.

32 **knoll'd**：rung.

36 **enforcement**：form of persuasion.

43 **upon command**：at your will,as it pleases you.

44 **wanting**：need. **minister'd**：supplied.

46 **Whiles**：while. **doe**：mother deer. **fawn**：young deer.

49 **suffic'd**：satisfied.

50 **Oppress'd**：weighed down. **weak**：enfeabling.

53 **waste**：consume.

54—55 **be bless'd**：may you be blessed. **comfort**：assistance.

56 把大千世界比喻成舞台。本剧上演于莎士比亚所属的宫内大臣剧团于1599年新建的"寰球剧院"(the Globe).该剧院的格言是"人人都是演员"(Totus mundus agit histrionem).

58 **woful pageants**：sorrowful scenes.

They have their exits and their entrances;
And one man in his time plays many parts,
His acts being seven ages. At first the infant,
Mewling and puking in the nurse's arms.
And then the whining school-boy, with his satchel,
And shining morning face, creeping like snail
Unwillingly to school. And then the lover,
Sighing like furnace, with a woful ballad
Made to his mistress' eyebrow. Then a soldier,
Full of strange oaths, and bearded like the pard,
Jealous in honour, sudden and quick in quarrel,
Seeking the bubble reputation
Even in the cannon's mouth. And then the justice,
In fair round belly with good capon lin'd,
With eyes severe, and beard of formal cut,
Full of wise saws and modern instances;
And so he plays his part. The sixth age shifts
Into the lean and slipper'd pantaloon,
With spectacles on nose and pouch on side,
His youthful hose well sav'd, a world too wide
For his shrunk shank; and his big manly voice,
Turning again toward childish treble, pipes
And whistles in his sound. Last scene of all,
That ends this strange eventful history,
Is second childishness and mere oblivion,
Sans teeth, sans eyes, sans taste, sans everything.

Re-enter ORLANDO, *with* ADAM.

DUKE S. Welcome. Set down your venerable burden.
And let him feed.

ORL. I thank you most for him.

ADAM. So had you need:
I scarce can speak to thank you for myself.

64 **His acts being seven ages**：全场演出按年龄可以分成七幕。

65 **Mewling**：crying. **puking**：vomiting.

66 **whining**：whimpering(呜咽声)。

69 **woful ballad**：sad poem.

70 **Made to**：dedicated to.

71 **pard**：leopard(形容胡须长且挺直，像豹的须)。

72 **Jealous in honour**：anxiously vigilant to protect his honour.

73—74 **Seeking...mouth**：甚至在炮口之下，寻求泡泡一样的虚名。

74 **justice**：justice of the peace(治安法官)，不一定谙熟法律，但能仲裁一般性案例，常由中年人担任，在香港译为"太平绅士"。

75 **capon**：熟鸡。 **lin'd**：filled.

76 **of formal cut**：cut with care (so as to suit an important man).

77 **saws**：maxims, proverbs. **modern instances**：commonplace examples.

79 **pantaloon**：feeble and foolish old man.原是意大利喜剧中穿扎腿长裤的滑稽老头。

80 **pouch**：purse.

81 **hose**：灯笼裤。 **well sav'd**：保存得很好的。 **a world too wide**：异常宽大。

82 **shrunk shank**：瘦缩的小腿。

83 **treble**：high-pitched voice.

84 **his**：its (voice's).

86 **childishness**：childhood. **mere oblivion**：utter forgetfulness.

87 **sans**〈法语〉：without.

1 **Set down...**：当时 Orlando 正肩背着 Adam，故云。 **venerable burden**：指 Adam.因其年老，品德又高，故云 venerable.

5 **So had you need**：You had the need to say the thanks for me.

6 **scarce**：scarcely.

DUKE S. Welcome; fall to: I will not trouble you
As yet, to question you about your fortunes.
Give us some music; and, good cousin, sing.

SONG

AMI. Blow, blow, thou winter wind.
Thou art not so unkind
As man's ingratitude;
Thy tooth is not so keen,
Because thou art not seen.
Although thy breath be rude.
Heigh-ho! sing heigh-ho! unto the green holly:
Most friendship is feigning, most loving mere folly.
Then, heigh-ho! the holly!
This life is most jolly.
Freeze, freeze, thou bitter sky,
That dost not bite so nigh
As benefits forgot:
Though thou the waters warp,
Thy sting is not so sharp
As friend remember'd not.
Heigh-ho! sing, heigh-ho! unto the green holly:
Most friendship is feigning, most loving mere folly.
Then heigh-ho! the holly!
This life is most jolly.

DUKE S. If that you were the good Sir Rowland's son,
As you have whisper'd faithfully you were,
And as mine eye doth his effigies witness
Most truly limn'd and living in your face,
Be truly welcome hither: I am the duke
That lov'd your father: the residue of your fortune,
Go to my cave and tell me. Good old man,

7 **fall to**：start eating.

8 **fortunes**：遭遇。

6 **rude**：harsh.

7 **Heigh-ho**：an expression of joy. **holly**：冬青类植物，叶有五刺角，结红果，圣诞节饰物，也是欢乐的象征。

8 **feigning**：deceiving.

12 **so nigh**：so close to the bone.

13 **benefits forgot**：forgotten benefits，受施而忘恩。

14 **warp**：cause to change the form (into ice).

21 **If that**：if.

23 **whisper'd**：Amiens 唱歌时，Orlando 在与老爵低声耳语。**faithfully**：assuringiy，convincingly.

24 **effigies**：likeness，features.

25 **limn'd**：portrayed.

27 **the residue of your fortune**：the rest of your story. 作下行 tell 的直接宾语。

Thou art right welcome as thy master is.
Support him by the arm. Give me your hand,
And let me all your fortunes understand.

[*Exeunt*.

29 **right**: very.

31 Let me know everything that has happened to you.

ACT III

SCENE I

—A Room in the Palace.

Enter DUKE FREDERICK, OLIVER, Lords, *and* Attendants.

DUKE F. Not seen him since! Sir, sir, that cannot be:
But were I not the better part made mercy,
I should not seek an absent argument
Of my revenge, thou present. But look to it:
Find out thy brother wheresoe'er he is;
Seek him with candle; bring him, dead or living,
Within this twelvemonth, or turn thou no more
To seek a living in our territory.
Thy lands and all things that thou dost call thine
Worth seizure, do we seize into our hands,
Till thou canst quit thee by thy brother's mouth
Of what we think against thee.

OLI. O that your highness knew my heart in this!
I never lov'd my brother in my life.

DUKE F. More villain thou. Well, push him out of doors;
And let my officers of such a nature
Make an extent upon his house and lands.
Do this expediently and turn him going.

[*Exeunt.*

SCENE II

—The Forest of Arden.

Enter ORLANDO, *with a paper*

ORL. Hang there, my verse, in witness of my love:

III.i

1 **Sir**：指 Oliver.一开场，公爵已与他谈话有时。 **him**：指公爵要捉拿的 Orlando，即 Oliver 的弟弟。

3 **the better part**：for the greater part. **made**：made of.

4 **absent**：who is not present.

4—5 **argument of my revenge**：subject for revenge.

5 **thou present**：thou being present，有你在场，意为本来大可拿你出气。 **look to it**：take care.

7 **Seek him with candle**：《圣经·新约·路加福音》第 15 章第 18 节记载一位妇女掉了一块钱，点上蜡烛在屋里仔细找寻。

8 **or**：otherwise. **turn**：return.

11 **Worth seizure**：值得没收，作上行 all things 的定语。

12 **quit thee**：acquit yourself. **mouth**：testimony.

13 **Of...**：(洗刷)我们对你的怀疑。

14 **my heart**：my real feelings.

18 **of such a nature**：competent in such matters.

19 **extent**：seizure in execution of an extent (a wit).

20 **turn him going**：send him on his way.

III.ii

a paper：a piece of paper.

And thou, thrice-crowned queen of night, survey With
thy chaste eye, from thy pale sphere above,
Thy huntress' name, that my full life doth sway.
O Rosalind! these trees shall be my books,
And in their barks my thoughts I'll character,
That every eye, which in this forest looks,
Shall see thy virtue witness'd everywhere.
Run, run, Orlando: carve on every tree
The fair, the chaste, and unexpressive she.

[*Exit*.

Enter CORIN *and* TOUCHSTONE.

COR. And how like you this shepherd's life, Master Touchstone?

TOUCH. Truly, shepherd, in respect of itself, it is a good life; but in respect that it is a shepherd's life, it is naught. In respect that it is solitary, I like it very well; but in respect that it is private, it is a very vile life. Now, in respect it is in the fields, it pleaseth me well; but in respect it is not in the court, it is tedious. As it is a spare life, look you, it fits my humour well; but as there is no more plenty in it, it goes much against my stomach. Hast any philosophy in thee, shepherd?

COR. No more but that I know the more one sickens the worse at ease he is; and that he that wants money, means, and content, is without three good friends; that the property of rain is to wet, and fire to burn; that good pasture makes fat sheep, and that a great cause of the night is lack of the sun; that he that hath learned no wit by nature nor art may complain of good breeding, or comes of a very dull kindred.

TOUCH. Such a one is a natural philosopher. Wast ever in court, shepherd?

COR. No, truly.

2 thrice-crowned queen of night：希腊、罗马神话中三位一体的女神。她在天上是月亮女神(Cynthia)，在凡间是贞洁和狩猎女神(Diana)，在冥间是女王(Proserpina).

3 sphere：圆穹，指月亮的轨迹。

4 Thy huntress' name：the name of Rosalind. Diana 既是狩猎女神，又是处女保护神，故 Orlando 以 Rosalind 为她的猎伴。 **full**：whole. **sway**：control；govern.

6 character：inscribe.

7 That：so that.

8 witness'd：spoken of.

10 unexpressive：inexpressible，indescribable. **she**：girl.

3 in respect of itself：in itself.

4 in respect that：in so far as.

5 naught：worthless.

6 private：lonely，cut off from the world.

8 spare：frugal.

9 humour：temperament. **but**：except.

13—14 wants：lacks. **means**：property. **content**：满足。

15 property：special quality. **fire**：前面省略 that of.

17 wit：knowledge.

18 nor art：nor by learning. **complain of**：lament the lack of.

19 dull kindred：unintelligent family.

20 natural philosopher：此词在 16 世纪用来称呼科学家，但 Touchstone 在玩弄 natural 的另一个含义"a born fool".

TOUCH. Then thou art damned.

COR. Nay, I hope.

TOUCH. Truly, thou art damned, like an ill-roasted egg, all on one side.

COR. For not being at court? Your reason.

TOUCH. Why, if thou never wast at court thou never sawest good manners; if thou never sawest good manners, then thy manners must be wicked; and wickedness is sin, and sin is damnation. Thou art in a parlous state, shepherd.

COR. Not a whit, Touchstone: those that are good manners at the court, are as ridiculous in the country as the behaviour of the country is most mockable at the court. You told me you salute not at the court, but you kiss your hands; that courtesy would be uncleanly if courtiers were shepherds.

TOUCH. Instance, briefly; come, instance.

COR. Why, we are still handling our ewes, and their fells, you know, are greasy.

TOUCH. Why, do not your courtier's hands sweat? and is not the grease of a mutton as wholesome as the sweat of a man? Shallow, shallow. A better instance, I say; come.

COR. Besides, our hands are hard.

TOUCH. Your lips will feel them the sooner: Shallow again. A more sounder instance; come.

COR. And they are often tarred over with the surgery of our sheep; and would you have us kiss tar? The courtier's hands are perfumed with civet.

TOUCH. Mostshallow man! Thou worms-meat, in respect of a good piece of flesh, indeed! Learn of the wise, and perpend: civet is of a baser birth than tar, the very uncleanly flux of a cat. Mend the instance, shepherd.

25—26 like an...one side：煎得一面焦而另一面生的鸡蛋。Corin 一贯在乡下生活，没有到过宫廷，因此 Touchstone 以 one-sided 讽喻。

29 manners：① deportment（举止）；②morals.

31 parlous：perilous 一词当时的拼法。

33 a whit：a bit.

36 salute：greet each other. **but you kiss**：without kissing.

39 Instance：proof. **briefly**：quickly.

40 still：contantly. **ewes**：female sheep.

41 fells：fleeces.

42 your：any.

48 more sounder：双重比较级在当时是常用的。

49 tarred over：涂满焦油（以焦油涂抹羊的伤口是当时一种土医法）。

51 civet：麝香。

52 worms-meat：meat only fit to be eaten by worms，是 Thou 的同位语。

52—53 in respect of：in comparison with. **Learn of**：learn from.

54 perpend：consider.

55 flux：secretion（分泌物）。 **cat**：civet cat. **Mend**：improve. **instance**：example，proof.

COR. You have too courtly a wit for me: I'll rest.

TOUCH. Wilt thou rest damned? God help thee, shallow man! God make incision in thee! thou art raw.

COR. Sir, I am a true labourer: I earn that I eat, get that I wear, owe no man hate, envy no man's happiness, glad of other men's good, content with my harm; and the greatest of my pride is to see my ewes graze and my lambs suck.

TOUCH. That is another simple sin in you, to bring the ewes and the rams together, and to offer to get your living by the copulation of cattle; to be bawd to a bell-wether, and to betray a she-lamb of a twelvemonth to a crooked-pated, old, cuckoldly ram, out of all reasonable match. If thou be'st not damned for this, the devil himself will have no shepherds: I cannot see else how thou shouldst'scape.

COR. Here comes young Master Ganymede, my new mistress's brother.

Enter ROSALIND, *reading a paper*.

ROS. From the east to western Ind,
No jewel is like Rosalind.
Her worth, being mounted on the wind,
Through all the world bears Rosalind.
All the pictures fairest lin'd
Are but black to Rosalind.
Let no face be kept in mind.
But the fair of Rosalind.

TOUCH. I'll rime you so, eight years together, dinners and suppers and sleeping hours excepted: it is the right butter-women's rank to market.

ROS. Out, fool!

57 **rest**：give up.

59 **make incision in**：cut in pieces.

60 **raw**：①生肉未煮的状态；②uneducated.

61 **that**：that which，下同。 **get**：earn.

62 **hate**：cause of hatred.

63 **content...harm**：patient with my misfortune.

66 **simple**：①foolish；②unashamed.

67 **offer**：dare，presume.

68—69 **bawd**：procure（娼主）。 **copulation**：交配。 **bell-wether**：挂铃的羊，头羊。 **of a twelvemonth**：yearling.

70 **crooked-pated**：①with crooked horno；②头上长角意为当王八的。 **cuckoldy**：当王八的，同 cuckoldly. **out of**：beyond the limit of.

71 **the devil**：前面省略 it must be because.

72 **will have no shepherds**：i.e. in hell. **else**：otherwise.

73 **'scape**：escape.

1 **east**：eastern. **Ind**：Indies，欧洲人在 15、16 世纪之交航海发现西印度群岛，以为这里就是印度；后到达东方，把印度和东南亚岛屿统称东印度。

3 **worth**：reputation.

4 **bears**：carries the fame of.

5 **fairest lin'd**：most beautifully drawn.

6 **to**：in comparison to.

8 **fair** (n.)：beauty.

9 **rime you so**：make rimes like these. **together**：without intermission.

11 **right**：just，reritable. **rank**：movement in line or file.

12 **Out**：quiet.

TOUCH. For a taste:—

If a hart do lack a hind,
Let him seek out Rosalind.
If the cat will after kind.
So be sure will Rosalind.
Winter-garments must be lin'd,
So must slender Rosalind.
They that reap must sheaf and bind.
Then to cart with Rosalind.
Sweetest nut hath sourest rind.
Such a nut is Rosalind.
He that sweetest rose will find
Must find love's prick and Rosalind.

This is the very false gallop of verses; why do you infect yourself with them?

ROS. Peace! you dull fool: I found them on a tree.

TOUCH. Truly, the tree yields bad fruit.

ROS. I'll graff it with you, and then I shall graff it with a medlar: then it will be the earliest fruit i' the country; for you'll be rotten ere you be half ripe, and that's the right virtue of the medlar.

TOUCH. You have said; but whether wisely or no, let the forest judge.

Enter CELIA, *reading a paper*.

ROS. Peace!
Here comes my sister, reading: stand aside.

CEL. Why should this a desert be?
For it is unpeopled? No;
Tongues I'll hang on every tree,
That shall civil sayings show.
Some, how brief the life of man

13 **For a taste**：as an example.

14 **hart**：male deer. **hind**：female deer.

16 **will after kind**：will go after its mate.

18 **lin'd**：①padded，stuffed；②mated.

20 **sheaf and bind**：gather (the wheat) into sheaves and tie them into bundles.

21 **to cart with**：① must be loaded on to a cart；②must be tied to a cart and whipped (as punishment for a prostitute).

22 **rind**：shell.

24 **will**：wishes to.

25 **prick**：①thorn；②penis.

26 **very false gallop of verses**：quite the worst kind of verse. Touchstone 把诗与劣马的步子相比。 **gallop**：pace.

26—27 **infect yourself with**：let yourself be troubled by.

31 **graff**：graft(嫁接)，you 与 yew 同音。

32 **medlar**：①一种一熟就烂的苹果；②谐 meddlar，an interfering person.

34 **right virtue**：true quality.

35 **said**：expressed one's opinion.

3 **desert**：lonely place.

4 **For**：because.

5 **Tongues**：writings.

6 **civil sayings**：sayings of civilized society.

Runs his erring pilgrimage,
That the stretching of a span
Buckles in his sum of age;
Some, of violated vows
'Twixt the souls of friend and friend:
But upon the fairest boughs,
Or at every sentence' end,
Will I Rosalinda write;
Teaching all that read to know
The quintessence of every sprite
Heaven would in little show.
Therefore Heaven Nature charg'd
That one body should be fill'd
With all graces wide enlarg'd.
Nature presently distill'd
Helen's cheek, but not her heart,
Cleopatra's majesty,
Atalanta's better part,
Sad Lucretia's modesty.
Thus Rosalind of many parts
By heavenly synod was devis'd
Of many faces, eyes, and hearts,
To have the touches dearest priz'd.
Heaven would that she these gifts should have,
And I to live and die her slave.

ROS. O most gentle pupiter! What tedious homily of love have you wearied your parishioners withal, and never cried, 'Have patience, good people!'

CEL. How now! Back, friends! Shepherd, go off a little; go with him, sirrah.

TOUCH. Come, shepherd, let us make an honourable retreat; though not with bag and baggage, yet with scrip and scrippage.

8 **his**: its. **erring pilgrimage**: wandering journey.

9 **span**: 手指伸开能达到的最大距离,一拃。

10 **Buckles in**: encloses. **sum of age**: length of life.

12 **'Twixt**: between.

15 **Rosalinda**: 在意大利文中的拼法 Rosalind,这样此行就与此段其他诗行一样有四个音步:

Will I | Rosa-| linda | write

17 **quintessence**: essence,purest form. **sprite**: spirit.

18 **in little**: on a small scale,in miniature.隐喻上帝以人类精华,荟萃于 Rosalind 娇小的身体。

19 **Heaven...charg'd**: heaven charged (ordered) Nature.

21 **wideenlarg'd**: that were extended everywhere.

22 **presently**: at once.

23 **Helen**: 希腊传说中最美的女人,但对丈夫(Menelaus)不忠,与特洛伊王子(Paris)私奔,引起希腊对特洛伊的战争。

24 **Cleopatra**: 埃及女王(纪元前 51—30 在位),以美貌与仪容著称。

25 **Atalanta**: 希腊神话中善跑的美女,求婚者如赛跑落后则被杀。后来 Hippomenes 在赛跑时一路上分段丢下三只金苹果,Atalanta 因拾金苹果而落后,不得不嫁给他。 **better part**: strong point,即善跑。

26 **Lucretia**: 莎士比亚长诗《鲁克丽丝受辱记》中的女主角,因为受辱而自尽。

28 **synod**: assembly. **devis'd**: made,composed.

30 **touches**: features. **priz'd**: valued.

31 **would**: wished.

33 **pupiter**: preacher. **homily**: sermon.

35 **'Have...people!'**: 教士布道时,对倦听的会众常用此语。

37 **sirrah**: 对下人的称呼。

39—40 **bag and baggage**: (成语)全部家当。 **scrip**: 皮做的小袋子,装钱或装烟丝。 **scrippage**: 为了与 baggage 相对称而杜撰的词。

[*Exeunt* CORIN *and* TOUCHSTONE.

CEL. Didst thou hear these verses?

ROS. O, yes, I heard them all, and more too; for some of them had in them more feet than the verses would bear.

CEL. That's no matter: the feet might bear the verses.

ROS. Ay, but the feet were lame, and could not bear themselves without the verse, and therefore stood lamely in the verse.

CEL. But didst thou hear without wondering, how thy name should be hanged and carved upon these trees?

ROS. I was seven of the nine days out of the wonder before you came; for look here what I found on a palm-tree: I was never so be-rimed since Pythagoras' time, that I was an Irish rat, which I can hardly remember.

CEL. Trow you who hath done this?

ROS. Is it a man?

CEL. And a chain, that you once wore, about his neck. Change you colour?

ROS. I prithee, who?

CEL. O Lord, Lord! it is a hard matter for friends to meet; but mountains may be removed with earthquakes, and so encounter.

ROS. Nay, but who is it?

CEL. Is it possible?

ROS. Nay, I prithee now, with most petitionary vehemence, tell me who it is.

CEL. O wonderful, wonderful, and most wonderful wonderful! and yet again wonderful! and after that, out of all whooping!

ROS. Good my complexion! dost thou think,

44 feet：①脚；②音步，即诗行中的音节组。

45 bear：①carry；②endure.

48 lame：①跛脚；②音步不当。

52 should be：came to be.

54—55 seven...wonder：英语中有"a nine days' wonder"的成语，意为 a short-lived surprise.Rosalind 说九天时间她已过了七天，表示已不感到新鲜。

56—57 Pythagoras' time：Pythagoras (c.580—500 B.C.)是古希腊哲学家，主灵魂轮回说。 **that**：when. **Irish rat**：英俗嘲笑爱尔兰人以念咒灭鼠。Rosalind 前世如当过爱尔兰老鼠，曾被人用韵文咒骂。

59 Trow you：do you know.

61 And a chain：and with a chain.

64 hard：difficult. **friends**：lovers.

66 encounter：前省略 friends may.

68 Is it possible that you need to be told?

69—70 petitionary vehemence：vehement petition，当时修辞方法，常可将修饰字与名词调换词类。

72—73 out of：beyond. **whooping**：hooping，expression of surprise.

74 Good my complexion：spare my blushing.

though I am caparison'd like a man, I have a doublet and hose in my disposition? One inch of delay more is a South sea of discovery; I prithee, tell me who is it quickly, and speak apace. I would thou couldst stammer, that thou mightst pour this concealed man out of thy mouth, as wine comes out of a narrow-mouth'd bottle; either too much at once, or none at all. I prithee, take the cork out of thy mouth, that I may drink thy tidings.

CEL. So you may put a man in your belly.

ROS. Is he of God's making? What manner of man? Is his head worth a hat, or his chin worth a beard?

CEL. Nay, he hath but a little beard.

ROS. Why, God will send more, if the man will be thankful. Let me stay the growth of his beard, if thou delay me not the knowledge of his chin.

CEL. It is young Orlando, that tripped up the wrestler's heels and your heart both, in an instant.

ROS. Nay, but the devil take mocking: speak, sad brow and true maid.

CEL. I' faith, coz, 'tis he.

ROS. Orlando?

CEL. Orlando.

ROS. Alas the day! what shall I do with my doublet and hose? What did he when thou sawest him? What said he? How looked he? Wherein went he? What makes he here? Did he ask for me? Where remains he? How parted he with thee, and when shalt thou see him again? Answer me in one word.

CEL. You must borrow me Gargantua's mouth first; 'tis a word too great for any mouth of this age's size. To say ay and no to these particulars is more than

75—76 caparison'd: dressed. **doublet and hose**: masculine nature(转喻,参见 II.iv 第 6—7 行)。

76—77 South sea of discovery: voyage of discovery in the South sea.莎士比亚时代,澳大利亚周围的 South sea 刚被发现。

78 apace: fast. **would**: wish.

83 tidings: news.

85 of God's making: ①真的男人,非为伪;②男子汉。与俗语 of tailor's making 相对称,后者为衣冠楚楚,但品质差。

86 worth: deserving of.

90 stay: wait for.

91 me: for me (dative). **his chin**: whose chin it is.

94 the devil take mocking: stop making fun of me.

94—95 sad brow and true maid: with a serious face and as an honest.

101—102 Wherein went he?: What clothes was he wearing? **makes he**: is he doing.

103 remains: dwells.

104—105 in one word: at once.下文 Celia 故意从字面上理解,说自己没有那么大的嘴。

106 Gargantua's mouth: Gargantua 是法国作家 Rabelais (c. 1494—c.1553)同名小说中的巨人主角,一口能吞下五个活人。该小说于 1532—1564 年分部出版,可见莎士比亚了解当代法国作品。

107—108 this age's size: the small size of people's mouths in our time. **particulars**: questions.

108 is more than: would take more time than it takes.

to answer in a catechism.

ROS. But doth he know that I am in this forest and in man's apparel? Looks he as freshly as he did the day he wrestled?

CEL. It is as easy to count atomies as to resolve the propositions of a lover; but take a taste of my finding him, and relish it with good observance. I found him under a tree, like a dropped acorn.

ROS. It may well be called Jove's tree, when it drops forth such fruit.

CEL. Give me audience, good madam.

ROS. Proceed.

CEL. There lay he, stretch'd along like a wounded knight.

ROS. Though it be pity to see such a sight, it well becomes the ground.

CEL. Cry 'holla!' to thy tongue, I prithee; it curvets unseasonably. He was furnish'd like a hunter.

ROS. O, ominous! he comes to kill my heart.

CEL. I would sing my song without a burden: thou bringest me out of tune.

ROS. Do you not know I am a woman? When I think, I must speak. Sweet, say on.

CEL. You bring me out. Soft! comes he not here?

ROS. 'Tis he: slink by, and note him.

Enter ORLANDO *and* JAQUES.

JAQ. I thank you for your company; but, good faith, I had as lief have been myself alone.

ORL. And so had I; but yet, for fashion' sake, I thank you too for your society.

JAQ. God be wi' you: let's meet as little as we can.

ORL. I do desire we may be better strangers.

109 **catechism**：基督教教义问答。

111 **freshly**：healthily.

113 **atomies**：speaks of dust.

113—114 **resolve**：answer. **propositions**：questions.

114 **take a taste of**：enjoy (the story of).

115 **observance**：attention.

116 **acorn**：fruit of the oak(橡树果实)。

117 **Jove's tree**：橡树乃树中之王，故云。

119 **audience**：hearing，attention.

121 **along**：at full length.

123—124 **becomes**：suits，adorns. **ground**：earth.

125 **'holla!'**：stop，要马停步的吆喝。

125 **curvets**：leaps around.

126 **unseasonably**：at the wrong time. 此处指 Rosalind 不停地插嘴。 **furnish'd**：dressed.

127 **heart**：与 hart(鹿)谐音，形成双关语。

128 **would**：wish I could. **without a burthen**：不用伴奏。意告 Rosalind 不要老是打断话头。

132 **bring me out**：put me off.

134 **slink by**：stop aside quietly. **note**：watch.

2 **as lief**：rather. **myself**：by myself.

4 **society**：company.

5 **be wi'**：be with.

JAQ. I pray you, mar no more trees with writing love-songs in their barks.

ORL. I pray you mar no more of my verses with reading them ill-favouredly.

JAQ. Rosalind is your love's name?

ORL. Yes, just.

JAQ. I do not like her name.

ORL. There was no thought of pleasing you when she was christened.

JAQ. What stature is she of?

ORL. Just as high as my heart.

JAQ. You are full of pretty answers. Have you not been acquainted with goldsmiths' wives, and conn'd them out of rings?

ORL. Not so; but I answer you right painted cloth, from whence you have studied your questions.

JAQ. You have a nimble wit: I think 'twas made of Atalanta's heels. Will you sit down with me? and we two will rail against our mistress the world, and all our misery.

ORL. I will chide no breather in the world but myself, against whom I know most faults.

JAQ. The worst fault you have is to be in love.

ORL. 'Tis a fault I will not change for your best virtue. I am weary of you.

JAQ. By my troth, I was seeking for a fool when I found you.

ORL. He is drowned in the brook:
look but in, and you shall see him.

JAQ. There I shall see mine own figure.

ORL. Which I take to be either a fool or a cipher.

JAQ. I'll tarry no longer with you. Farewell,

8 **mar**：injure；spoil.

11 **ill-favouredly**：badly，in an uncomely manner.

13 **just**（adv.）：exactly.

17 **stature**：height.

20—21 **conn'd them out of rings**：learned those pretty answers from the mottos engraved inside their rings.

22 **right**：true，genuine. **painted cloth**：painted wall-hangings.当时挂在墙上装饰用的壁毯，上面常画有人物，嘴里引出说的话，像气球一样。这里意为我的答和你的问同源于壁毯。

24 **nimble wit**：quick mind.

25 **Atalanta's heels**：见第 95 页注 25。

28 **breather**：one who breathes，living person.

31 **change**：exchange.

33 **troth**：faith.

39 **cipher**：the figure "O"，i.e.nothing.

40 **tarry**：stay.

good Signior Love.

ORL. I am glad of your departure. Adieu, good Monsieur Melancholy. [*Exit* JAQUES.

ROS. I will speak to him like a saucy lackey, and under that habit play the knave with him. Do you hear, forester?

ORL. Very well: what would you?

ROS. I pray you, what is't o'clock?

ORL. You should ask me, what time o' day; there's no clock in the forest.

ROS. Then there is no true lover in the forest; else sighing every minute and groaning every hour would detect the lazy foot of Time as well as a clock.

ORL. And why not the swift foot of Time? had not that been as proper?

ROS. By no means, sir. Time travels in divers paces with divers persons. I'll tell you who Time ambles withal, who Time trots withal, who Time gallops withal, and who he stands still withal.

ORL. I prithee, who doth he trot withal?

ROS. Marry, he trots hard with a young maid between the contract of her marriage and the day it is solemnized; if the interim be but a se'nnight, Time's pace is so hard that it seems the length of seven year.

ORL. Who ambles Time withal?

ROS. With a priest that lacks Latin, and a rich man that hath not the gout; for the one sleeps easily because he cannot study, and the other lives merrily because he feels no pain; the one lacking the burden of lean and wasteful learning, the other knowing no burden of heavy tedious penury. These Time ambles withal.

ORL. Who doth he gallop withal?

ROS. With a thief to the gallows; for though he go as softly as foot can fall he thinks himself too soon there.

41 Signior〈意大利语〉：先生。

44 lackey：servant.

45 habit：dress，outward appearance. **knave**：serving-boy，false fellow.

47 what would you：what do you want.

56—57 divers：different. **paces**：speeds.通常指马的步子，注意下文一些词如 ample，trot，gallop 等都是形容马的。

59 withal：with.

61 trots hard：goes at an uncomfortable，uneven trot.

62 solemnized：publicly completed.

63 interim：interval. **se'-nnight**：week.

66 lacks Latin：does not understand Latin，拉丁文是钻研宗教必须会的文字，天主教会用的圣经全是拉丁文译本。

67 gout：痛风病。

69—70 lean and wasteful learning：study that makes a man go thin and waste away.

74 softly：slowly.

ORL. Who stays it still withal?

ROS. With lawyers in the vacation; for they sleep between term and term, and then they perceive not how Time moves.

ORL. Where dwell you, pretty youth?

ROS. With this shepherdess, my sister; here in the skirts of the forest, like fringe upon a petticoat.

ORL. Are you native of this place?

ROS. As the cony, that you see dwell where she is kindled.

ORL. Your accent is something finer than you could purchase in so removed a dwelling.

ROS. I have been told so of many: but indeed an old religious uncle of mine taught me to speak, who was in his youth an inland man; one that knew courtship too well, for there he fell in love. I have heard him read many lectures against it; and I thank God, I am not a woman, to be touched with so many giddy offences as he hath generally taxed their whole sex withal.

ORL. Can you remember any of the principal evils that he laid to the charge of women?

ROS. There were none principal; they were all like one another as half-pence are; every one fault seeming monstrous till his fellow fault came to match it.

ORL. I prithee, recount some of them.

ROS. No, I will not cast away my physic, but on those that are sick. There is a man haunts the forest, that abuses our young plants with carving 'Rosalind' on their barks; hangs odes upon hawthorns, and elegies on brambles; all, forsooth, deifying the name of Rosalind: If I could meet that fancy-monger, I would give him some good counsel, for he seems to have the quotidian of love upon him.

ORL. I am he that is so love-shaked. I pray you,

76 vacation：法院两次开庭之间的假期。开庭期称 term.

81 skirts：outskirts. **fringe**：花边。

83 cony：rabbit.

84 kindled：born.

86 purchase：acquire. **removed**：remote.

87—88 of：by. **religious**：i.e.member of some religious order.

89—90 inland：living near the capital and centre of culture. **courtship**：① life at court；②wooing.

90—91 read many lectures：deliver many admonitions.

92—93 touched：tainted. **giddy offences**：capricions faults. **generally**：in general. **taxed**：accused.

95 laid to the charge of：accused...of.

98 his：its.

100 physic：medicine.此句参见《圣经·新约·马太福音》第 9 章第 12 节：They that are whole have no need of a physician，but they that are sick.

101 haunts：前省略 who.

103—104 hawthorns：山楂树。 **elegies**：哀歌。 **brambles**：荆棘。 **forsooth**：indeed. **deifying**：treating...as a god or goddess.

105 fancy-monger：dealer in love.

106 quotidian：malarian fevel.

108 love-shaked：shaken by the fever of love.

tell me your remedy.

ROS. There is none of my uncle's marks upon you: he taught me how to know a man in love; in which cage of rushes I am sure you are not prisoner.

ORL. What were his marks?

ROS. A lean cheek, which you have not: a blue eye and sunken, which you have not; an unquestionable spirit, which you have not; a beard neglected, which you have not; but I pardon you for that, for, simply, your having in beard is a younger brother's revenue. Then, your hose should be ungartered, your bonnet unbanded, your sleeve unbuttoned, your shoe untied, and everything about you demonstrating a careless desolation. But you are no such man: you are rather point-device in your accoutrements; as loving yourself than seeming the lover of any other.

ORL. Fair youth, I would I could make thee believe I love.

ROS. Me believe it! you may as soon make her that you love believe it; which, I warrant, she is apter to do than to confess she does; that is one of the points in the which women still give the lie to their consciences. But, in good sooth, are you he that hangs the verses on the trees, wherein Rosalind is so admired?

ORL. I swear to thee, youth, by the white hand of Rosalind, I am that he, that unfortunate he.

ROS. But are you so much in love as your rimes speak?

ORL. Neither rime nor reason can express how much.

ROS. Love is merely a madness, and, I tell you, deserves as well a dark house and a whip as madmen do; and the reason why they are not so punished and

111 my uncle's marks：signs (of love-sickness) described by my uncle.

112—113 cage of rushes：cage made of straw，意为情网很容易冲破。

115 blue eye：眼圈发黑，常因失眠引起。

116 unquestionable spirit：unwillingness to talk.

118 for that：for your not having a beard. **simply**：frankly. **your having in**：what you have in the way of.

119 a younger...revenue：像(无继承权的)小兄弟的收入一样少。

122 careless desolation：despair that makes you careless of your appearance.

123 point-device：designed to the point (to the smallest detail).

124—125 as...other：you look more like a man who loves himself than the love of another person.

126 would：wish.

129—130 apter：readier. **to do**：to believe.

131 in the which：in which，中世纪英语中 which 为名词，可加冠词。 **still**：always.

131—132 give... consciences：lie about their real feelings. **sooth**：truth. **he**：man.

139 reason：plain language.

141 merely：entirely.

142 a dark house and a whip：中世纪认为疯子系有鬼魂附身，将其关在暗室鞭打，可以驱鬼而恢复神志。

143 they：lovers.

cured is, that the lunacy is so ordinary that the whippers are in love too. Yet I profess curing it by counsel.

ORL. Did you ever cure any so?

ROS. Yes, one; and in this manner. He was to imagine me his love, his mistress; and I set him every day to woo me: at which time would I, being but a moonish youth, grieve, be effeminate, changeable, longing and liking; proud, fantastical, apish, shallow, inconstant, full of tears, full of smiles, for every passion something, and for no passion truly anything, as boys and women are, for the most part, cattle of this colour; would now like him, now loathe him; then entertain him, then forswear him; now weep for him, then spit at him; that I drave my suitor from his mad humour of love to a living humour of madness; which was, to forswear the full stream of the world, and to live in a nook merely monastic. And thus I cured him; and this way will I take upon me to wash your liver as clean as a sound sheep's heart, that there shall not be one spot of love in't.

ORL. I would not be cured, youth.

ROS. I would cure you, if you would but call me Rosalind, and come every day to my cote and woo me.

ORL. Now, by the faith of my love, I will: tell me where it is.

ROS. Go with me to it and I'll show it you; and by the way you shall tell me where in the forest you live. Will you go?

ORL. With all my heart, good youth.

ROS. Nay, you must call me Rosalind. Come, sister, will you go? [*Exeunt*.

144 **ordinary**: common.

145—146 **profess**: claim to have the skill of. **counsel**: advice.

149 **set him**: give him the task.

150 **moonish**: changeable like the moon.

152 **fantastical**: full of fancies. **apish**: affected like an ape.

153—154 **for...anything**: showing some signs of every emotion, but feeling no emotion sincerely.

155 **cattle of this colour**: creatures of this kind.

156—157 **entertain**: receive kindly. **forswear**: refuse.

157—158 **that**: with the result that. **drave**: drove.

158—159 **mad humour of love**: mad state of mind caused by love. **living humour of madness**: actual state of madness.

159—161 **forswear...monastic**: 抛弃人世,遁入空门。 **nook**: hidden place. **merely monastic**: completely like a monastery (without women).

162 **wash your liver**: 当时认为人的激情都发自肝脏。

163 **that**: so that.

165 **would not**: do not want to.

167 **cote**: cottage.

171—172 **by the way**: on our way there.

SCENE III

—Another Part of the Forest.

Enter TOUCHSTONE *and* AUDREY; JAQUES *behind.*

TOUCH. Come apace, good Audrey: I will fetch up your goats, Audrey. And how, Audrey? am I the man yet? doth my simple feature content you?

AUD. Your features! Lord warrant us! what features?

TOUCH. I am here with thee and thy goats, as the most capricious poet, honest Ovid, was among the Goths.

JAQ. [*Aside*] O knowledge ill-inhabited, worse than Jove in a thatch'd house!

TOUCH. When a man's verses cannot be understood, nor a man's good wit seconded with the forward child Understanding, it strikes a man more dead than a great reckoning in a little room. Truly, I would the gods had made thee poetical.

AUD. I do not know what 'poetical' is. Is it honest in deed and word? Is it a true thing?

TOUCH. No, truly, for the truest poetry is the most feigning; and lovers are given to poetry, and what they swear in poetry may be said as lovers they do feign.

AUD. Do you wish then that the gods had made me poetical?

TOUCH. I do, truly; for thou swearest to me thou art honest: now, if thou wert a poet, I might have some hope thou didst feign.

AUD. Would you not have me honest?

TOUCH. No, truly, unless thou wert hard-favour'd; for honesty coupled to beauty is to have honey a sauce to sugar.

III.iii

1 **apace**：quickly.

2—3 **the man**：the man you (Audrey) choose to marry. **feature**：person.

4 **Your features!**：Audrey 没有受过教育，不懂 features 一词的意思。 **warrant**：protect；save.

7 **capricious poet**：fanciful poet. capricious 源于拉丁文“caper”，意为“he-goat”(公羊)，因此 capricious poet 又可解释为 goat-poet. **Ovid**：奥维德(公元前 43—公元 18)，古罗马诗人，莎士比亚对他的诗极为赞赏。

8 **Goths**：古罗马时期欧洲日耳曼族的一支野蛮民族，Ovid 曾被放逐到该民族地区。Goths 的发音在伊丽莎白时代与 goats 相同，因此 Touchstone 这段话又可理解为“goat-poet...among the goats”.

9 **ill-inhabited**：ill-lodged(不得其所)。

10 **Jove...house!**：据罗马神话，天帝 Jove(即 Jupiter)与信使神 Mercury 曾乔装到农家夫妇 Philemon 与 Baucis 家中做客，受到竭诚招待。后来 Jove 将其茅舍化为寺院。

12 **seconded with**：followed by，supported by.

12—13 **foward child Understanding**：clever child called Understanding. i.e. the listener's understanding.

13—14 **a great...room**：an extravagant bill for humble food in a small tavern(小酒馆开出了大账单)。此处可能影射当代剧作家 Christopher Marlowe(1564—1593)，他在一家小酒店因为付账与人口角械斗时被杀(第 13 行：strike a man...dead).

19 **feigning**：①pretending；②imaginative. **given to**：in the habit of expressing their feelings in.

20 **as**：前省略 that.

26 **honest**：chaste.

27—28 **hard-favour'd**：ugly-faced. **coupled to**：joined with.

28—29 **have honey...sugar**：糖里加蜜。i.e. too much of a good thing.

JAQ. [*Aside*.] A material fool.

AUD. Well, I am not fair, and therefore I pray the gods make me honest.

TOUCH. Truly, and to cast away honesty upon a foul slut were to put good meat into an unclean dish.

AUD. I am not a slut, though I thank the gods I am foul.

TOUCH. Well, praised be the gods for thy foulness! sluttishness may come hereafter. But be it as it may be, I will marry thee; and to that end I have been with Sir Oliver Martext, the vicar of the next village, who hath promised to meet me in this place of the forest, and to couple us.

JAQ. [*Aside*.] I would fain see this meeting.

AUD. Well, the gods give us joy!

TOUCH. Amen. A man may, if he were of a fearful heart, stagger in this attempt; for here we have no temple but the wood, no assembly but horn-beasts. But what though? Courage! As horns are odious, they are necessary. It is said, 'many a man knows no end of his goods:' right; many a man has good horns, and knows no end of them. Well, that is the dowry of his wife; 'tis none of his own getting. Horns? Even so. Poor men alone? No, no; the noblest deer hath them as huge as the rascal. Is the single man therefore blessed? No: as a walled town is more worthier than a village, so is the forehead of a married man more honourable than the bare brow of a bachelor; and by how much defence is better than no skill, by so much is a horn more precious than to want. Here comes Sir Oliver.

Enter SIR OLIVER MARTEXT.

Sir Oliver Martext, you are well met: will you dispatch

30 material：full of matter or ideas.

33—34 foul slut：plain and lazy woman.

38—39 be it as it may be：in any case；anyway. **to that end**：for that purpose.

40 Sir Oliver Martext：当时对牧师都可以尊称为 Sir. Martext 由 mar(＝spoil)与 text(＝holy text)两词组成，隐含离经叛道之义。

42 couple：marry.

43 fain：willingly.

46 stagger：waver，hesitate.

48 what though：what of that. **As**：though. **horns**：在伊丽莎白时代，当王八称为头上长角。

49—50 knows no end of：does not know the extent of.

50 good horns：good cause to wear horns (be a cuckold).

51 knows no end of them：does not know how faithless his wife is.

52—53 Even so：Very true. **Poor... alone**：Is it true of poor men only?

54 rascal：inferior animal in a herd (of deer). **single**：unmarried.

55—56 a walled... village：城有城墙防御，胜似没有任何防御的村子。

57 bare brow：没有角的，就像四周没有围墙的村子。

58 defence：skill in seif-defence.

59 want：lack one.

1 well met：welcome. **dispatch**：settle business with，i.e.marry.

us here under this tree, or shall we go with you to your chapel?

SIR OLI. Is there none here to give the woman?

TOUCH. I will not take her on gift of any man.

SIR OLI. Truly, she must be given, or the marriage is not lawful.

JAQ. [*Coming forward.*] Proceed, proceed: I'll give her.

TOUCH. Good even, good Master What-ye-call't: how do you, sir? You are very well met: God'ild you for your last company: I am very glad to see you: even a toy in hand here, sir: nay, pray be covered.

JAQ. Will you be married, motley?

TOUCH. As the ox hath his bow, sir, the horse his curb, and the falcon her bells, so man hath his desires; and as pigeons bill, so wedlock would be nibbling.

JAQ. And will you, being a man of your breeding, be married under a bush, like a beggar? Get you to church, and have a good priest that can tell you what marriage is: this fellow will but join you together as they join wainscot; then one of you will prove a shrunk panel, and like green timber, warp, warp.

TOUCH. [*Aside.*] I am not in the mind but I were better to be married of him than of another: for he is not like to marry me well, and not being well married, it will be a good excuse for me hereafter to leave my wife.

JAQ. Go thou with me, and let me counsel thee.

TOUCH. Come, sweet Audrey:
We must be married, or we must live in bawdry. Farewell, good Master Oliver: not

O sweet Oliver!

4 give the woman：西方礼仪，婚礼上经常由父亲将女儿“交付”给新郎。

5 on gift of：as a gift from.

10 even：evening. **What-ye -call't**：whatever your name is.

11—12 'ild：yield，reward. **last company**：指他们上次见面(II. vii，第 12 行以下)。

12 even：just. **toy**：trifle.

13 pray be covered：please put on your hat.

14 motley：穿拼花衣者，fool.

15 bow：yoke(轭)。

16 curb：马衔。 **bells**：挂在猎鹰腿上的铃。

17 bill(v.)：caress each other with their beaks (bills).

17—18 nibbling：biting gently，kissing.

22 join wainscot：钉腰墙板。

23—24 shrunk panel：没有晒干，因此会干缩的木板。 **green**：not properly dried. **warp**：变形。

25—26 not...but：两个否定，构成肯定，I am inclined to think that. **were better...another**：would do better being married by Sir Oliver Martext than by another priest.

27 like：likely.

32 in bawdry：in sin.

34—40 Touchstone 所唱的歌，前三句为现成的歌谣，后三句是他自己凑的。

O brave Oliver!
Leave me not behind thee:
but,—
Wind away,
Begone, I say,
I will not to wedding with thee.

[*Exeunt* JAQUES, TOUCHSTONE, *and* AUDREY.

SIR OLI. 'Tis no matter: ne'er a fantastical knave of them all shall flout me out of my calling.

[*Exit*.

SCENE IV

——*Another Part of the Forest*.

Enter ROSALIND *and* CELIA.

ROS. Never talk to me: I will weep.

CEL. Do, I prithee; but yet have the grace to consider that tears do not become a man.

ROS. But have I not cause to weep?

CEL. As good cause as one would desire; therefore weep.

ROS. His very hair is of the dissembling colour.

CEL. Something browner than Judas's; marry, his kisses are Judas's own children.

ROS. I' faith, his hair is of a good colour.

CEL. An excellent colour: your chestnut was ever the only colour.

ROS. And his kissing is as full of sanctity as the touch of holy bread.

CEL. He hath bought a pair of cast lips of Diana: a nun of winter's sisterhood kisses not more religiously; the very ice of chastity is in them.

ROS. But why did he swear he would come this morning, and comes not?

38 Wind：wander，go.

40 to wedding：前面省略 go.

42 flout：mock，jeer. **calling**：vocation（职业）。

III.iv

1 Never：don't.

3 become：suit，其时 Rosalind 仍女扮男装。

7 dissembling colour：deceitful colour，i.e. red colour.当时相信出卖耶稣（Jesus）的犹大（Judas）头发是红的。

8 Something：a little. **browner**：比红色更深一些。伊丽莎白时代惯用 brown 指红发。

8—9 his kisses...children：犹大以与耶稣接吻，暴露并出卖了耶稣，因此犹大之吻成了背叛的代名词。

11 your chestnut：the colour of the chestnut.这里 your 属较随便的口语用法，无所有格意味。

14 holy bread：圣餐面包，即在教堂举行仪式和分给信徒的不发酵的小面包片，象征耶稣的肉身。

15 cast：discarded，此句意为经他吻过，就像经 Diana 吻过一样。Diana 是罗马神话中的月亮女神和贞操女神。

16 of winter's sisterhood：devoted to cold and barren chastity.

17 ice：coldness. **them**：his lips.

CEL. Nay, certainly, there is no truth in him.

ROS. Do you think so?

CEL. Yes: I think he is not a pick-purse nor a horse-stealer; but for his verity in love, I do think him as concave as a covered goblet or a worm-eaten nut.

ROS. Not true in love?

CEL. Yes, when he is in;
but I think he is not in.

ROS. You have heard him swear downright he was.

CEL. 'Was' is not 'is;' besides, the oath of a lover is no stronger than the word of a tapster; they are both the confirmers of false reckonings. He attends here in the forest on the duke your father.

ROS. I met the duke yesterday and had much question with him. He asked me of what parentage I was; I told him, of as good as he; so he laughed, and let me go. But what talk we of fathers, when there is such a man as Orlando?

CEL. O, that's a brave man! he writes brave verses, speaks brave words, swears brave oaths, and breaks them bravely, quite traverse, athwart the heart of his lover; as a puisny tilter, that spurs his horse but on one side, breaks his staff like a noble goose. But all's brave that youth mounts and folly guides. Who comes here?

Enter CORIN.

COR. Mistress and master, you have oft inquir'd After the shepherd that complain'd of love,
Who you saw sitting by me on the turf,
Praising the proud disdainful shepherdess
That was his mistress.

CEL. Well, and what of him?

20 **truth**：faithfulness.

22 **pick-purse**：thief who steals purses.

23 **verity**：truthfulness.

23—24 **concave**：hollow. **covered goblet**：合上盖的空酒杯（按常例，goblet 只有在不用时才合上盖）。

27 **in**：in love.

31 **tapster**：waiter at an inn who serves wine. **they**：lover and tapster.

32 **confimers of false reckonings**：witnesses to false statements (bills).

34 **question**：conversation.

37 **what**：for what purpose.

39 **brave**：fine.Celia 连续使用此词，明显含有讽刺意味。

41 **traverse** (adv.)：across，横向。 **athwart**：across.

42 **puisny**：puny，petty. **tilter**：刺枪比赛之骑士。tilting 为中世纪骑士比武方式，骑马的武士戴全副盔甲，持长枪比武，将对方戳翻下马者得胜。

43—44 **staff**：spear，lance.马刺只踢马的一侧，马跑偏了，矛或横向，就在对方胸前甲胄上折断，此为败绩。 **goose**：fool. **all's**：all love is. **mounts** (v.t.)：骑，驾驭。

COR. If you will see a pageant truly play'd,
Between the pale complexion of true love
And the red glow of scorn and proud disdain,
Go hence a little, and I shall conduct you,
If you will mark it.

ROS. O! come, let us remove:
The sight of lovers feedeth those in love.
Bring us to this sight, and you shall say
I'll prove a busy actor in their play. [*Exeunt*.

SCENE V

—Another Part of the Forest.

Enter SILVIUS *and* PHEBE.

SIL. Sweet Phebe, do not scorn me; do not, Phebe:
Say that you love me not, but say not so
In bitterness. The common executioner,
Whose heart the accustom'd sight of death makes hard,
Falls not the axe upon the humbled neck
But first begs pardon: will you sterner be
Than he that dies and lives by bloody drops?

Enter ROSALIND, CELIA, *and* CORIN, *behind*.

PHE. I would not be thy executioner:
I fly thee, for I would not injure thee.
Thou tell'st me there is murder in mine eye:
'Tis pretty, sure, and very probable,
That eyes, that are the frail'st and softest things,
Who shut their coward gates on atomies,
Should be call'd tyrants, butchers, murderers!
Now I do frown on thee with all my heart;
And, if mine eyes can wound, now let them kill thee;
Now counterfeit to swound; why now fall down;
Or, if thou canst not, O! for shame, for shame,
Lie not, to say mine eyes are murderers.
Now show the wound mine eye hath made in thee;

7 pageant: drama, scene.

11 mark: watch.

12 remove: move away.

III.v

3 common: public. **executioner**: 行刑刽子手。

5 Falls: lets fall, 在此作及物动词。 **humbled**: bowed.

6 But first begs: without first begging.

7 dies and lives: spends his whole life; earns his living. **by bloody drops**: i.e. by being an executioner.

10 fly: flee from, avoid.

12 pretty: fine, ingenious(含讽刺意)。

14 coward: cowardly. **gates**: eyelids. **on**: against. **atomies**: specks of dust.

18 counterfeit: pretend.

20 Lie not: do not tell lies.

Scratch thee but with a pin, and there remains
Some scar of it, lean but upon a rush,
The cicatrice and capable impressure
Thy palm some moment keeps; but now mine eyes,
Which I have darted at thee, hurt thee not,
Nor, I am sure, there is not force in eyes
That can do hurt.

SIL. O dear Phebe,
If ever,—as that ever may be near.—
You meet in some fresh cheek the power of fancy,
Then shall you know the wounds invisible
That love's keen arrows make.

PHE. But, till that time
Come not thou near me: and, when that time comes,
Afflict me with thy mocks, pity me not;
As, till that time I shall not pity thee.

ROS. [*Advancing*.] And why, I pray you? Who might be your mother,
That you insult, exult, and all at once,
Over the wretched? What though you have no beauty,—
As by my faith, I see no more in you
Than without candle may go dark to bed,—
Must you be therefore proud and pitiless?
Why, what means this? Why do you look on me?
I see no more in you than in the ordinary
Of nature's sale-work. 'Od's my little life!
I think she means to tangle my eyes too.
No, faith, proud mistress, hope not after it:
'Tis not your inky brows, your black silk hair,
Your bugle eyeballs, nor your cheek of cream,
That can entame my spirits to your worship.
You foolish shepherd, wherefore do you follow her.
Like foggy south puffing with wind and rain?
You are a thousand times a properer man

23 **rush**：灯心草。

24 **cicatrice**：scar, mark. **capable**：sensible. **impressure**：impression.

28 **hurt** (n.)：harm.

30 **ever**：any time.

31 **fresh cheek**：new face. **power of fancy**：power to draw your love.

33 **love's keen arrows**：据希腊、罗马神话，爱神丘比特(Cupid)为长翅膀、持弓箭的小男孩，中其箭者即堕入情网。

40 **all at once**：at the same time.

42 **no more**：no more light (i.e. beauty).

45 **look on**：stare at.

46 **ordinary**：ordinary run.

47 **sale-work**：ready-made work. **'Od's**：God save.

48 **tangle**：entangle.

51 **bugle**：bead (commonly made of black glass).

52 **entame**：tame, enslave. **your worship**：worship of you.

54 **south**：south wind. 在英国，南风经常带来雾和雨。 **puffing**：blowing. **wind and rain**：既指自然界的风雨，又指叹息和眼泪。

55 **properer**：more handsome.

Than she a woman: 'tis such fools as you
That make the world full of ill-favour'd children:
'Tis not her glass, but you, that flatters her;
And out of you she sees herself more proper
Than any of her lineaments can show her.
But, mistress, know yourself: down on your knees,
And thank heaven, fasting, for a good man's love:
For I must tell you friendly in your ear,
Sell when you can; you are not for all markets.
Cry the man mercy; love him; take his offer:
Foul is most foul, being foul to be a scoffer.
So take her to thee, shepherd. Fare you well.

PHE. Sweet youth, I pray you, chide a year together;
I had rather hear you chide than this man woo.

ROS. He's fallen in love with her foulness, and she'll fall in love with my anger. If it be so, as fast as she answers thee with frowning looks, I'll sauce her with bitter words. Why look you so upon me?

PHE. For no ill will I bear you.

ROS. I pray you, do not fall in love with me, For I am falser than vows made in wine:
Besides, I like you not. If you will know my house, 'Tis at the tuft of olives here hard by.
Will you go, sister? Shepherd, ply her hard.
Come, sister. Shepherdess, look on him better,
And be not proud: though all the world could see,
None could be so abused in sight as he.
Come, to our flock.

[*Exeunt* ROSALIND, CELIA, *and* CORIN.

PHE. Dead shepherd, now I find thy saw of might:
'Who ever lov'd that lov'd not at first sight?'

SIL. Sweet Phebe,—

PHE. Ha! what sayst thou, Silvius?

57 **ill-favour'd**：plain,ugly.

58 **glass**：mirror.

59 **out of you**：looking out of you (as out of a mirror).

60 **lineaments**：容貌。

62 **fasting**：taking no food,as a sign of repentance.

63 **friendly**：as a friend. **in your ear**：privately.

65 **Cry...mercy**：beg one's pardon.

66 **Foul**：ugliness，ugly person. **foul**：ugly.

68—69 **chide**：scold. **together**：Without stopping.

71—72 **He's...anger**：第一分句是对 Phebe 说的；第二分句是对 Silvius 说的。

73 **sauce** (v.t.)：scold sharply,made one smart.

77 **falser...wine**：比喝醉时发的誓更靠不住。

79 **tuft**：clump (of trees). **hard by**：near by.

80 **ply**：work at steadily.

81 **look on**：treat.

83 **abused in sight**：deceived by the sight (thinking what he sees is beautiful).

85 **Dead shepherd**：在牧歌中惯称诗人为 shepherd.

86 **"Who...sight?"**：此行引自马娄的叙事长诗 *Hero And Leander*(《希罗与里昂德》)。马娄死于 1593 年，此诗未完成。由 George Chapman 续完，于 1598 年发表。

SIL. Sweet Phebe, pity me.

PHE. Why, I am sorry for thee, gentle Silvius.

SIL. Wherever sorrow is, relief would be:
If you do sorrow at my grief in love,
By giving love your sorrow and my grief
Were both extermin'd.

PHE. Thou hast my love: is not that neighbourly?

SIL. I would have you.

PHE. Why, that were covetousness.
Silvius, the time was that I hated thee;
And yet it is not that I bear thee love:
But since that thou canst talk of love so well,
Thy company, which erst was irksome to me,
I will endure, and I'll employ thee too;
But do not look for further recompense
Than thine own gladness that thou art employ'd.

SIL. So holy and so perfect is my love,
And I in such a poverty of grace,
That I shall think it a most plenteous crop
To glean the broken ears after the man
That the main harvest reaps: loose now and then
A scatter'd smile, and that I'll live upon.

PHE. Know'st thou the youth that spoke to me erewhile?

SIL. Not very well, but I have met him oft;
And he hath bought the cottage and the bounds
That the old carlot once was master of.

PHE. Think not I love him, though I ask for him.
'Tis but a peevish boy; yet he talks well;
But what care I for words? yet words do well,
When he that speaks them pleases those that hear.
It is a pretty youth: not very pretty:
But, sure, he's proud; and yet his pride becomes him:
He'll make a proper man: The best thing in him

91 Wherever sorrow is felt,a desire to give relief should follow,此处的 sorrow 系对 Phebe 上行所说的 sorry 而发。

94 **were**：would be. **extermin'd**：put an end to.

95 **neighbourly**：《圣经·新约·马太福音》第 22 章第 39 节，"Thou shalt love thy neighbour as thyself."

97 **covetousness**：贪婪。《圣经·旧约·出埃及记》第 20 章第 17 节，"Thou shalt not covet...anything that is thy neighhour's."

101 **erst**：formerly. **irksome**：annoying.

103 **recompense**：repayment.

106 **poverty**：need. **grace**：favour.

107 **plenteous crop**：bumper harvest.

108 **glean**：collect. **ears**：ears of corn.参见《圣经·旧约·路得记》第 2 章故事。

109 **loose**：set free.

110 **scatter'd**：stray,漫不经心的。

111—112 **erewhile**：just now.

114 **bounds**：land.

115 **carlot**：peasant.

116 **ask for**：ask about.

117 **peevish**：silly.

121 **becomes**：suits.

122 **proper**：handsome.

Is his complexion; and faster than his tongue
Did make offence his eye did heal it up.
He is not very tall; yet for his years he's tall:
His leg is but so-so; and yet 'tis well:
There was a pretty redness in his lip,
A little riper and more lusty red
Than that mix'd in his cheek; 'twas just the difference
Betwixt the constant red and mingled damask.
There be some women, Silvius, had they mark'd him
In parcels as I did, would have gone near
To fall in love with him; but, for my part,
I love him not nor hate him not; and yet
Have more cause to hate him than to love him:
For what had he to do to chide at me?
He said mine eyes were black and my hair black;
And, now I am remember'd, scorn'd at me.
I marvel why I answer'd not again:
But that's all one; omittance is no quittance.
I'll write to him a very taunting letter,
And thou shalt bear it: wilt thou, Silvius?

SIL. Phebe, with all my heart.

PHE. I'll write it straight;
The matter's in my head and in my heart:
I will be bitter with him and passing short.
Go with me, Silvius. [*Exeunt*.

124 make offence: hurt, wound.

126 but so-so: only passable.

128 riper: fuller. **lusty**: bright.

129 that: the redness.

130 constant red: all-red; brightly red(大红)。 **mingled damask**: 一种淡红色的玫瑰。

131 mark'd: observed.

132 In parcels: in detail; part by part.

136 what...do: what right did he have.

138 am remember'd: am reminded, recall.

139 marvel: wonder. **again**: back.

140 that's all one: it doesn't matter. **omittance**: omission, i.e. not answering back. **quittance**: discharging from debt, pardoning.

146 passing: very.

ACT IV

SCENE I

—The Forest of Arden.

Enter ROSALIND, CELIA, *and* JAQUES.

JAQ. I prithee, pretty youth, let me be better acquainted with thee.

ROS. They say you are a melancholy fellow.

JAQ. I am so; I do love it better than laughing.

ROS. Those that are in extremity of either are abominable fellows, and betray themselves to every modern censure worse than drunkards.

JAQ. Why, 'tis good to be sad and say nothing.

ROS. Why then, 'tis good to be a post.

JAQ. I have neither the scholar's melancholy, which is emulation; nor the musician's, which is fantastical; nor the courtier's, which is proud; nor the soldier's, which is ambitious; nor the lawyer's, which is politic; nor the lady's, which is nice; nor the lover's, which is all these: but it is a melancholy of mine own, compounded of many simples, extracted from many objects, and, indeed, the sundry contemplation of my travels, which, by often rumination, wraps me in a most humorous sadness.

ROS. A traveller! By my faith, you have great reason to be sad. I fear you have sold your own lands to see other men's; then, to have seen much and to have nothing, is to have rich eyes and poor hands.

JAQ. Yes, I have gained my experience.

ROS. And your experience makes you sad: I had rather have a fool to make me merry than experience

IV.i

5 **are...either**: go to either extreme.

6 **modern**: ordinary.

8 **sad**: ① serious; ②heavy, stiff.

9 **post**: 木桩。

10 **melancholy**: ill-temper.

11 **emulation**: envy. **fantastical**: fanciful.

13—14 **politic**: crafty. **nice**: fastidious.

16 **simples**: ingredients.

17 **sundry contemplation**: various thoughts.

18 **often**: frequent. **rumination**: deep thinking. **humorous**: moody.

to make me sad: and to travel for it too!

Enter ORLANDO.

ORL. Good day, and happiness, dear Rosalind!

JAQ. Nay then, God be wi' you, an you talk in blank verse. [*Exit*.

ROS. Farewell, Monsieur Traveller: look you lisp, and wear strange suits, disable all the benefits of your own country, be out of love with your nativity, and almost chide God for making you that countenance you are; or I will scarce think you have swam in a gondola. Why, how now, Orlando! where have you been all this while? You a lover! An you serve me such another trick, never come in my sight more.

ORL. My fair Rosalind, I come within an hour of my promise.

ROS. Break an hour's promise in love! He that will divide a minute into a thousandth parts, and break but a part of the thousandth part of a minute in the affairs of love, it may be said of him that Cupid hath clapped him o' the shoulder, but I'll warrant him heart-whole.

ORL. Pardon me, dear Rosalind.

ROS. Nay, an you be so tardy, come no more in my sight: I had as lief be wooed of a snail.

ORL. Of a snail!

ROS. Ay, of a snail; for though he comes slowly, he carries his house on his head; a better jointure, I think, than you make a woman: besides, he brings his destiny with him.

ORL. What's that?

ROS. Why, horns; that such as you are fain to be beholding to your wives for: but he comes armed in his fortune and prevents the slander of his wife.

2—3 an：if. **blank verse**：每行五音步的无韵诗。莎士比亚剧本中大部分诗行属这种体例，Orlando 与 Rosalind 打招呼时用的也是这种诗行：Good 'day | and 'hap- | pi'ness | dear 'Ro- | sa'lind |

4—8 look...gondola：莎士比亚借 Rosalind 之口，讽刺当时一些人从欧洲旅行回来后，连说话穿衣都要模仿外国人。

4—5 look you：see to it that you. **lisp**：speak affectedly with a foreign accent. **disable**：disparage.

6 nativity：nationality.

7 countenance：face. **you are**：you have.

8 scarce：scarcely. **swam**：floated. **gondola**：意大利威尼斯城水上交通所用的平底游艇。当时威尼斯是欧洲文化中心，吸引了许多旅游者。

10 serve：play.

17—18 clapped...shoulder：只射中肩膀，因心脏未被射中，故未真的陷入情网。

22 as lief：rather. **of**：by.

25 his house：指蜗牛壳。 **jointure**：marriage settlement（丈夫在结婚时承诺授予妻子的财产）。

29 horns：参见 III.iii 第 48 行。 **fain**：inclined.

30—31 comes armed：指来的时候头上就长了角。 **prevents**：anticipates.

ORL. Virtue is no horn-maker; and my Rosalind is virtuous.

ROS. And I am your Rosalind?

CEL. It pleases him to call you so; but he hath a Rosalind of a better leer than you.

ROS. Come, woo me, woo me; for now I am in a holiday humour, and like enough to consent. What would you say to me now, an I were your very very Rosalind?

ORL. I would kiss before I spoke.

ROS. Nay, you were better speak first, and when you were gravelled for lack of matter, you might take occasion to kiss. Very good orators, when they are out, they will spit; and for lovers lacking,—God warn us! —matter, the cleanliest shift is to kiss.

ORL. How if the kiss be denied?

ROS. Then she puts you to entreaty, and there begins new matter.

ORL. Who could be out, being before his beloved mistress?

ROS. Marry, that should you, if I were your mistress; or I should think my honesty ranker than my wit.

ORL. What, of my suit?

ROS. Not out of your apparel, and yet out of your suit. Am not I your Rosalind?

ORL. I take some joy to say you are, because I would be talking of her.

ROS. Well, in her person I say I will not have you.

ORL. Then in mine own person I die.

ROS. No, faith, die by attorney. The poor world is almost six thousand years old, and in all this time there was not any man died in his own person, *videlicet*,

36 **leer**: face.

38 **humour**: mood. **like enough**: very likely.

42 **were better**: had better.

43 **gravelled**: (of a boat) run aground on gravel.搁浅。

44 **occasion**: opportunity. **out**: at a loss for words.

45 **warn**: protect.

46 **cleanliest shift**: most adroitly way out.cleanliest 还与上文 spit 相映成趣(接吻比吐痰干净得多)。

48 **to entreaty**: to plead with her.

50 **before**: in the presence of.

53—54 **honesty...wit**: 德有余而才不足。 **ranker**: greater.

55 **of my suit**: Will I be out of my suit? (求婚失败。)

56 **Not...suit**: suit 既指 apparel,又指 wooing, Rosalind 即以此打趣。

60 **in her person**: on her behalf.

63 **by attorney**: by proxy(请人代理)。

64 **six thousand years old**: 伊丽莎白时代的人根据《圣经》推算出来的数字。

in a love-cause. Troilus had his brains dashed out with a Grecian club; yet he did what he could to die before, and he is one of the patterns of love. Leander, he would have lived many a fair year, though Hero had turned nun, if it had not been for a hot mid-summer night; for, good youth, he went but forth to wash him in the Hellespont, and being taken with the cramp was drowned; and the foolish coroners of that age found it was 'Hero of Sestos.' But these are all lies: men have died from time to time, and worms have eaten them, but not for love.

ORL. I would not have my right Rosalind of this mind; for, I protest, her frown might kill me.

ROS. By this hand, it will not kill a fly. But come, now I will be your Rosalind in a more coming-on disposition; and ask me what you will, I will grant it.

ORL. Then love me, Rosalind.

ROS. Yes, faith will I, Fridays and Saturdays and all.

ORL. And wilt thou have me?

ROS. Ay, and twenty such.

ORL. What sayest thou?

ROS. Are you not good?

ORL. I hope so.

ROS. Why then, can one desire too much of a good thing? —Come, sister, you shall be the priest and marry us. —Give me your hand, Orlando. What do you say, sister?

ORL. Pray thee, marry us.

CEL. I cannot say the words.

ROS. You must begin, —'Will you, Orlando'—

CEL. Go to. —Will you, Orlando, have to wife this Rosalind?

ORL. I will.

65—66 *videlicet*〈拉丁语〉：namely. **in a love-cause**：because of love. **Troilus**：特洛伊国王 Priam 之子，被希腊大将 Achilles 打死，他曾与 Cressida 相爱，后来 Cressida 负心，另觅新欢。

67 **did...before**：他在早先也曾寻死觅活，但没有死于爱情。

68 **patterns**：models. **Leander**：古希腊传说中的一位青年，为了与情人 Hero 幽会，每天晚上游过 Hellespont 海峡，有一晚因遇上风暴而淹死。Rosalind 则对此重加穿凿，以证实她的看法。

69 **many a fair year**：many happy years. **turned nun**：become a priestess (of the tenple of Venus in Sestos).

71 **him**：himself.

73 **coroners**：验尸官。有的版本作"chroniclers"（史家）。**found**：gave the verdict. **it**：the cause of death.

76—77 **right**：real. **mind**：opinion. **protest**：declare.

79—80 **coming-on**：agreeable.

94 **Pray thee**：Please.

95 主持婚礼有一套固定的话要说，Celia 称她不会。

97 **Go to**：That is enough.

ROS. Ay, but when?

ORL. Why, now; as fast as she can marry us.

ROS. Then you must say, 'I take thee, Rosalind, for wife.'

ORL. I take thee, Rosalind, for wife.

ROS. I might ask you for your commission; but, I do take thee, Orlando, for my husband: there's a girl goes before the priest; and, certainly, a woman's thought runs before her actions.

ORL. So do all thoughts; they are winged.

ROS. Now tell me how long you would have her after you have possessed her?

ORL. For ever and a day.

ROS. Say 'a day,' without the 'ever.' No, no, Orlando; men are April when they woo, December when they wed: maids are May when they are maids, but the sky changes when they are wives. I will be more jealous of thee than a Barbary cock-pigeon over his hen; more clamorous than a parrot against rain; more new-fangled than an ape; more giddy in my desires than a monkey: I will weep for nothing, like Diana in the fountain, and I will do that when you are disposed to be merry; I will laugh like a hyen, and that when thou art inclined to sleep.

ORL. But will my Rosalind do so?

ROS. By my life, she will do as I do.

ORL. O! but she is wise.

ROS. Or else she could not have the wit to do this: the wiser, the waywarder: make the doors upon a woman's wit, and it will out at the casement; shut that, and 'twill out at the key-hole; stop that, 'twill fly with the smoke out at the chimney.

ORL. A man that hath a wife with such a wit, he might say, 'Wit, whither wilt?'

105 按例我可以问你凭什么娶我(因为当时 Celia 还没有问 Rosalind 是否愿意嫁给 Orlando). **commission**: legal authority.

106—107 **there's...priest**: Rosalind 指自己未等牧师发问就答应嫁给 Orlando. **goes before**: anticipates.

112 **For...day**: for ever and ever.

117 **Barbary cock-pigeon**: 一种雄鸽,据说配偶盯得很紧。Barbary 系北非洲海岸地名。 **hen**: hen-pigeon.

118 **against rain**: before it rains.

118—119 **new-fangled**: delighted by change or novelty. **giddy**: variable(反复无常)。

120 **Diana...fountain**: 喷泉常以 Diana 雕像作为装饰,喷水时就像她在哭泣。

122 **hyen**: hyena,鬣狗,叫时声如狂笑。

128 **waywarder**: more wilful. **make**: shut.

129 **out**: go out.

133 **'whither wilt?'**: where will you go.这句话常用来制止一个说话太多的人,参考 I.ii 第 54 行。

ROS. Nay, you might keep that check for it till you met your wife's wit going to your neighbour's bed.

ORL. And what wit could wit have to excuse that?

ROS. Marry, to say she came to seek you there. You shall never take her without her answer, unless you take her without her tongue. O! that woman that cannot make her fault her husband's occasion, let her never nurse her child herself, for she will breed it like a fool.

ORL. For these two hours, Rosalind, I will leave thee.

ROS. Alas! dear love, I cannot lack thee two hours.

ORL. I must attend the duke at dinner: by two o'clock I will be with thee again.

ROS. Ay, go your ways, go your ways; I knew what you would prove, my friends told me as much, and I thought no less: that flattering tongue of yours won me: 'tis but one cast away, and so, come, death! Two o'clock is your hour?

ORL. Ay, sweet Rosalind.

ROS. By my troth, and in good earnest, and so God mend me, and by all pretty oaths that are not dangerous, if you break one jot of your promise or come one minute behind your hour, I will think you the most pathetical break-promise, and the most hollow lover, and the most unworthy of her you call Rosalind, that may be chosen out of the gross band of the unfaithful. Therefore, beware my censure, and keep your promise.

ORL. With no less religion than if thou wert indeed my Rosalind: so, adieu.

134 **check**：rebuke.

137 第一个 wit 作“才情”解，第二个 wit 作“有才情的妻子”解。

139 **Marry**：by tbe Virgin Mary.

141 **take...tongue**：割去她的舌头。

142 **her husband's occasion**：a chance to find fault with her husband.

143 **breed**：rear, bring up.

147 **lack**：do without.

152 **prove**：prove to be.

154 **'tis...away**：it is just one more girl deserted.

158 **mend**：correct. **pretty**：fine（带讽刺意味）。

159 **dangerous**：i.e. dangerous to break.

161 **pathetical**：miserable. **break-promise**：breaker of promise. **hollow**：insincere.

163 **gross band**：entire number.

164 **beware**：beware of.

166 **religion**：faithfulness.

ROS. Well, Time is the old justice that examines all such offenders, and let Time try. Adieu.

[*Exit* ORLANDO.

CEL. You have simply misused our sex in your love-prate. we must have your doublet and hose plucked over your head, and show the world what the bird hath done to her own nest.

ROS. O coz, coz, coz, my pretty little coz, that thou didst know how many fathom deep I am in love! But it cannot be sounded: my affection hath an unknown bottom, like the bay of Portugal.

CEL. Or rather, bottomless; that as fast as you pour affection in, it runs out.

ROS. No; that same wicked bastard of Venus, that was begot of thought, conceived of spleen, and born of madness, that blind rascally boy that abuses every one's eyes because his own are out, let him be judge how deep I am in love. I'll tell thee, Aliena, I cannot be out of the sight of Orlando: I'll go find a shadow and sigh till he come.

CEL. And I'll sleep. [*Exeunt*.

SCENE II

—Another Part of the Forest.

Enter JAQUES, Lords, *and* Foresters.

JAQ. Which is he that killed the deer?

FIRST LORD. Sir, it was I.

JAQ. Let's present him to the duke, like a Roman conqueror, and it would do well to set the deer's horns upon his head for a branch of victory. Have you no song, forester, for this purpose?

SECOND LORD. Yes, sir.

JAQ. Sing it; 'tis no matter how it be in tune so it make noise enough.

168 justice：judge.

169 try：be the judge.

170—171 simply：utterly. **misused**：abused；disgraced. **love-prate**：foolish talk about love. **plucked over**：stripped off.

172—173 show... nest：show that the person who has abused woman is herself a woman.参考英谚 It is a foul bird that defiles its own nest.

174 that：I wish that.

176 sounded：measured in depth.

180 bastard of Venus：指爱神 Cupid，他是 Venus 同 Mercury 偷情所生。Rosalind 既要他判断她对 Orlando 的深情，又因他使情人受罪而责骂他。

181—182 begot...madness：因忧郁而感孕，因冲动而受胎，因疯狂而降生。 **thought**：melancholy. **spleen**：impulse.

182 abuses：deceives；deludes.

183 his...out：he himself is blind.

185 shadow：shade.

IV.ii

既然 Rosalind 须等待两个小时，这一场成为第一、三场之间极为短暂的过渡。伊丽莎白时代观众最喜欢嘲弄男人头上长角（即当王八），这一场中的歌就是迎合这种趣味。

3—4 Roman conqueror：罗马的凯旋将军。

5 branch of victory：胜利的桂冠。同时又指鹿角，因为鹿角的形状恰似树杈。

6 purpose：occasion.

8 how...tune：whether it is sung well. **so**：provided that.

8—9 make...enough：is loud enough.

SONG

What shall he have that kill'd the deer?
His leather skin and horns to wear.
Then sing him home.

[*The rest shall bear this burden*.

Take thou no scorn to wear the horn;
It was a crest ere thou wast born:
Thy father's father wore it,
And thy father bore it:
The horn, the horn, the lusty horn
Is not a thing to laugh to scorn.

[*Exeunt*.

SCENE III

—Another Part of the Forest.

Enter ROSALIND *and* CELIA.

ROS. How say you now? Is it not past two o'clock? And here much Orlando!

CEL. I warrant you, with pure love and a troubled brain, he hath ta'en his bow and arrows, and is gone forth to sleep. Look, who comes here.

Enter SILVIUS.

SIL. My errand is to you, fair youth.
My gentle Phebe did bid me give you this:

[*Giving a letter*.

I know not the contents; but, as I guess
By the stern brow and waspish action
Which she did use as she was writing of it,
It bears an angry tenour: pardon me;
I am but as a guiltless messenger.

ROS. Patience herself would startle at this letter,
And play the swaggerer:
bear this, bear all:

11 **His**：its.

13 ***bear this burden***：指上一行，在歌中是重复句，其余人需合唱。

14 **Take...scorn**：Don't be ashamed.

15 **crest**：原意为"鸡冠"，这里作"顶饰"。

18 **lusty**：joyous：merry.

IV.iii

2 **here...Orlando!**：（反语）这儿哪有奥兰多的人影！

3—5 Celia 讥笑 Orlando 爽约，就像猎手煞有介事地准备好弓箭，结果只是去睡觉而已。

11 **stern brow**：fierce look. **waspish**：spiteful，virulent wasp，是一种会蜇人的蜂。

13 **tenour**：substance，message.

15 **Patience**：拟人化的"忍耐"之神。 **startle**：start.

16 **swaggerer**：someone ready to have a quarrel.

17 **bear...all**：if one can bear this，one can bear anything.

She says I am not fair; that I lack manners;
She calls me proud, and that she could not love me
Were man as rare as Phœnix. 'Od's my will!
Her love is not the hare that I do hunt:
Why writes she so to me? Well, shepherd, well,
This is a letter of your own device.

SIL. No, I protest, I know not the contents: Phebe did write it.

ROS. Come, come, you are a fool,
And turn'd into the extremity of love.
I saw her hand: she has a leathern hand,
A freestone-colour'd hand; I verily did think
That her old gloves were on, but 'twas her hands:
She has a housewife's hand;
but that's no matter:
I say she never did invent this letter;
This is a man's invention, and his hand.

SIL. Sure, it is hers.

ROS. Why, 'tis a boisterous and a cruel style;
A style for challengers; Why, she defies me, Like Turk to Christian: woman's gentle brain Could not drop forth such giant-rude invention,
Such Ethiop words, blacker in their effect
Than in their countenance. Will you hear the letter?

SIL. So please you, for I never heard it yet; Yet heard too much of Phebe's cruelty.

ROS. She Phebes me. Mark how the tyrant writes. [*Reads*.]

Art thou god to shepherd turn'd.
That a maiden's heart hath burn'd?

Can a woman rail thus?

SIL. Call you this railing?

ROS. [*reads*.]

18 **fair**：beautiful.

20 **as...phœnix**：像凤凰一样稀少。相传世界仅有一只凤凰。历五百年后自焚。在灰烬中重获新生。 **'Od's ... will**：as God's will is my will.

23 **device**：invention.

27 **turn'd**：has fallen.

28 **leathern**：rough-skinned.

29 **freestone -colour'd**：砂石颜色的；灰黄色。

34 **hand**：handwriting.

37—38 **Like...Christian**：中世纪时，土耳其的穆斯林教徒占领耶路撒冷，引起欧洲的基督教徒十字军东征。

38 **drop forth**：produce.

39 **giant-rude**：immensely rude.

40 **Ethiop**：Ethiopian，black. **blacker**：more terrible.

41 **countenance**：appearance(信的字面是黑色的)。

44 **Phebes me**：writes to me in her own style，treats me with her kind of cruelty.

46—47 Are you a god who has changed himself into a shepherd.

Why, thy godhead laid apart.
Warr'st thou with a woman's heart?

Did you ever hear such railing?

Whiles the eye of man did woo me,
That could do no vengeance to me.

Meaning me a beast.

If the scorn of your bright eyne
Have power to raise such love in mine,
Alack! in me what strange effect
Would they work in mild aspect.
Whiles you chid me, I did love;
How then might your prayers move!
He that brings this love to thee
Little knows this love in me;
And by him seal up thy mind;
Whether that thy youth and kind
Will the faithful offer take
Of me and all that I can make;
Or else by him my love deny.
And then I'll study how to die.

SIL. Call you this chiding?

CEL. Alas, poor shepherd!

ROS. Do you pity him? no, he deserves no pity. Wilt thou love such a woman? What, to make thee an instrument, and play false strains upon thee! Not to be endured! Well, go your way to her, for I see love hath made thee a tame snake, and say this to her: that if she love me, I charge her to love thee: if she will not, I will never have her, unless thou entreat for her. If

53 **godhead**：divine nature. **laid apart**：put aside.

54 **Warr'st thou with**：do you make war against.

57 **That**：that kind of wooing. **vengeance**：harm.

60 **eyne**：eyes.为押韵而用的古拼法。

63 **they**：your eyes. **in mild aspect**：favourably. aspect 为占星术术语，指星辰对人的影响。

66 **love**：love-letter.

68 **by him**：with him as your messenger. **seal...mind**：send a sealed letter to let me know your mind.

69 **youth and kind**：youthful nature.

71 **make**：offer.

77—78 **What**：感叹词。 **to make thee**：making you（指 Silvius）. **instrument**：① tool；②musical instrument. **play false strains**：play falsehood.

you be a true lover, hence, and not a word, for here comes more company. [*Exit* SILVIUS.

Enter OLIVER.

OLI. Good morrow, fair ones. Pray you if you know,
Where in the purlieus of this forest stands
A sheepcote fenc'd about with olive-trees?

CEL. West of this place, down in the neighbour bottom:
The rank of osiers by the murmuring stream
Left on your right hand brings you to the place.
But at this hour the house doth keep itself;
There's none within.

OLI. If that an eye may profit by a tongue,
Then should I know you by description;
Such garments, and such years: 'The boy is fair,
Of female favour, and bestows himself
Like a ripe sister: but the woman low,
And browner than her brother.' Are not you
The owner of the house I did inquire for?

CEL. It is no boast, being ask'd, to say, we are.

OLI. Orlando doth commend him to you both, And to that youth he calls his Rosalind
He sends this bloody napkin. Are you he?

ROS. I am: what must we understand by this?

OLI. Some of my shame; if you will know of me What man I am, and how, and why, and where
This handkercher was stain'd.

CEL. I pray you, tell it.

OLI. When last the young Orlando parted from you
He left a promise to return again
Within an hour; and, pacing through the forest,
Chewing the food of sweet and bitter fancy,

83 **hence**：go away.

85 **morrow**：morning.

86 **purlieus**：borders.

88—89 **neighbour bottom**：neighbouring valley.

90 **rank of osiers**：row of willow trees.

91 **Left...hand**：left behind on your right hand，修饰 rank 的分词短语。

92 **doth...itself**：is empty.

94 If my eyes can profit by what I have been told.

95 **know**：recognize. **description**：从下文可知，Orlando 向 Oliver 描述了她俩的形象。

97 **female favour**：feminine features. **bestows**：conducts.

98 **ripe**：elder. **low**：short.

101 **being ask'd**：作状语，意思是"既蒙下问"，属 dangling participle 结构。

102 **commend him**：send his greetings.

104 **napkin**：handkerchief.

106 **Some...shame**：something I am ashamed of. **know of**：learn from.

113 **fancy**：love.

Lo, what befell! He threw his eye aside,
And mark what object did present itself:
Under an oak, whose boughs were moss'd with age,
And high top bald with dry antiquity,
A wretched ragged man, o'ergrown with hair,
Lay sleeping on his back: about his neck
A green and gilded snake had wreath'd itself,
Who with her head nimble in threats approach'd
The opening of his mouth; but suddenly,
Seeing Orlando, it unlink'd itself,
And with indented glides did slip away
Into a bush; under which bush's shade
A lioness, with udders all drawn dry,
Lay couching, head on ground, with catlike watch,
When that the sleeping man should stir; for 'tis
The royal disposition of that beast
To prey on nothing that doth seem as dead:
This seen, Orlando did approach the man,
And found it was his brother, his elder brother.

CEL. O! I have heard him speak of that same brother;
And he did render him the most unnatural
That liv'd 'mongst men.

OLI. And well he might so do,
For well I know he was unnatural.

ROS. But, to Orlando: did he leave him there,
Food to the suck'd and hungry lioness?

OLI. Twice did he turn his back and purpos'd so; But
kindness, nobler ever than revenge.
And nature, stronger than his just occasion,
Made him give battle to the lioness,
Who quickly fell before him: in which hurtling
From miserable slumber I awak'd.

CEL. Are you his brother?

115 **befell**: happened. **threw his eye**: glaced.

117 **moss'd**: covered with moss.

118 **bald**: without leaves. **dry antiquity**: old age that causes things to dry up.

121 **gilded**: gold-coloured. **wreath'd**: curled.

124 **unlink'd**: uncoiled.

125 **indeated glides**: zigzag gliding.

127 **udders...dry**: 乳房全被幼狮吸得干瘪,指母狮正在饥饿状态。

129 **When that**: for the time when.

130 **royal**: noble.

136 **render him**: describe him as. **unnatural**: devoid of natural feeling(不念手足之情)。

140 **to**: with regard to.

141 **suck'd**: 被吸干乳汁的。

142 **purpos'd so**: intended to do so.

143 **kindness**: generosity.

144 **occasion**: cause.

146 **hurtling**: noisy struggle.

ROS. Was it you he rescu'd?

CEL. Was't you that did so oft contrive to kill him?

OLI. 'Twas I; but 'tis not I. I do not shame
To tell you what I was, since my conversion
So sweetly tastes, being the thing I am.

ROS. But, for the bloody napkin?

OLI. By and by.
When from the first to last, betwixt us two,
Tears our recountments had most kindly bath'd,
As how I came into that desert place:—
In brief, he led me to the gentle duke,
Who gave me fresh array and entertainment,
Committing me unto my brother's love;
Who led me instantly unto his cave.
There stripp'd himself; and here, upon his arm
The lioness had torn some flesh away,
Which all this while had bled; and now he fainted,
And cried, in fainting, upon Rosalind.
Brief, I recover'd him, bound up his wound;
And, after some small space, being strong at heart,
He sent me hither, stranger as I am,
To tell this story, that you might excuse
His broken promise; and to give this napkin,
Dy'd in his blood, unto the shepherd youth
That he in sport doth call his Rosalind.

CEL. [ROSALIND *swoons*.] Why, how now, Ganymede! sweet Ganymede!

OLI. Many will swoon when they do look on blood.

CEL. There is more in it. Cousin! Ganymede!

OLI. Look, he recovers.

ROS. I would I were at home.

CEL. We'll lead you thither.
I pray you, will you take him by the arm?

150 **contrive**：plot.

152 **'Twas... I**：那是过去的我，但不是现在的我。 **do not shame**：am not ashamed.

153 **conversion**：change of character(改过自新)。

154 **being...am**：being the man I am，作整个句子的状语。

155—156 **for**：what about. **By and by**：I shall tell you soon.

157—158 这两行的主语是 tears，谓语是 had bath'd，宾语是 our recountments. When from...(自始至终)和 betwixt (between)...两个短语均作状语。 **recountments**：accounts of what has happened. **kindly**：in a natural way.

157—163 这七行的主谓语为 he led me.以下四行句法不清。表示快速叙述，有些语无伦次。

159 **As**：such as.

161 **array**：clothes. **entertainment**：food and drink.

162 **Committing me unto**：placing me in the care of.

164 **here**：Oliver 说话时在自己手臂上指示 Orlando 受伤的地方。

168 **Brief**：in brief. **recover'd**：revived.

169 **space**：amount of time.

170 **as**：though.

171 **that**：so that.

174 **in sport**：jokingly；playfully.

175 **how now**：what is the matter.

178 **Cousin**：Celia 在惊慌中忘了 Rosalind 假扮的身份。

OLI. Be of good cheer, youth. You a man!
You lack a man's heart.

ROS. I do so, I confess it. Ah, sirrah! a body would think this was well counterfeited. I pray you, tell your brother how well I counterfeited. Heigh-ho!

OLI. This was not counterfeit: there is too great testimony in your complexion that it was a passion of earnest.

ROS. Counterfeit, I assure you.

OLI. Well then, take a good heart and counterfeit to be a man.

ROS. So I do; but, i' faith, I should have been a woman by right.

CEL. Come; you look paler and paler: pray you, draw homewards. Good sir, go with us.

OLI. That will I, for I must bear answer back
How you excuse my brother, Rosalind.

ROS. I shall devise something. But, I pray you, commend my counterfeiting to him. Will you go?

[*Exeunt*.

187 Heigh-ho：真逗。

189—190 passion of earnest：genuine feeling.

192 take...heart：振作起来。

197 draw：withdraw.

199 How you excuse：whether you forgive. **Rosalind**：Oliver, like Orlando, is pretending that Ganymede is Rosalind.

200—201 commend：put in a good word for.

ACT V

SCENE I

— The Forest of Arden .

Enter TOUCHSTONE *and* AUDREY.

TOUCH. We shall find a time, Audrey: patience, gentle Audrey.

AUD. Faith, the priest was good enough, for all the old gentleman's saying.

TOUCH. A most wicked Sir Oliver, Audrey; a most vile Martext. But, Audrey, there is a youth here in the forest lays claim to you.

AUD. Ay, I know who 'tis: he hath no interest in me in the world. Here comes the man you mean.

Enter WILLIAM.

TOUCH. It is meat and drink to me to see a clown. By my troth, we that have good wits have much to answer for: we shall be flouting; we cannot hold.

Will. Good even, Audrey.

AUD. God ye good even, William.

Will. And good even to you, sir.

TOUCH. Good even, gentle friend. Cover thy head, cover thy head: nay, prithee, be covered. How old are you, friend?

Will. Five-and-twenty, sir.

TOUCH. A ripe age. Is thy name William?

Will. William, sir.

TOUCH. A fair name. Wast born i' the forest here?

Will. Ay, sir, I thank God.

TOUCH. 'Thank God;' a good answer. Art rich?

V.i

1 **a time**：i.e., a time to get married.

4 **old...saying**：指 Jaques 说的话。

5 **Sir Oliver**：指 Sir Oliver Maxtext.

7 **lays claim to**：who asserts his right to(认为你属于他)。

8 **interest in**：claim on.

10 **meat and drink**：something enjoyable. **clown**：idiot, country fellow.

11—12 **have much...for**：are greatly to blame. **we...flouting**：we are given to jeering at others. **hold**：restrain ourselves.

14 **God...even**：God give you a good evening.

16 **Cover...head**：put on your bat. William 出于尊敬，摘掉了帽子。注意在这一场中，Touchstone 不时摹仿宫廷中达官贵人的口吻，对 William 居高临下，以 thou 相称(第 30 行)。

24 **Art rich**：are you rich?

WILL. Faith, sir, so so.

TOUCH. 'So so' is good, very good, very excellent good: and yet it is not; it is but so so. Art thou wise?

WILL. Ay, sir, I have a pretty wit.

TOUCH. Why, thou sayest well. I do now remember a saying, 'The fool doth think he is wise, but the wise man knows himself to be a fool.' The heathen philosopher, when he had a desire to eat a grape, would open his lips when he put it into his mouth; meaning thereby that grapes were made to eat and lips to open. You do love this maid?

WILL. I do, sir.

TOUCH. Give me your hand. Art thou learned?

WILL. No, sir.

TOUCH. Then learn this of me: to have, is to have; for it is a figure in rhetoric, that drink, being poured out of a cup into a glass, by filling the one doth empty the other; for all your writers do consent that *ipse* is he: now, you are not *ipse*, for I am he.

WILL. Which he, sir?

TOUCH. He, sir, that must marry this woman. Therefore, you clown, abandon,—which is in the vulgar, leave,—the society,—which in the boorish is, company,— of this female,— which in the common is, woman; which together is, abandon the society of this female, or, clown, thou perishest; or, to thy better understanding, diest; or, to wit, I kill thee, make thee away, translate thy life into death, thy liberty into bondage. I will deal in poison with thee, or in bastinado, or in steel; I will bandy with thee in faction; I will o'er-run thee with policy; I will kill thee a hundred and fifty ways: therefore tremble, and depart.

AUD. Do, good William.

26 So so：moderately.

29 pretty wit：good intelligence.

32 heathen philosopher：异教哲学家。Touchstone 此处并不专指某人，可能是为了自炫博学，也可能 Williams 当时正张大嘴巴听他说话，被他顺便取笑。

38 learned：educated.

40 of me：from.

41 figure in rhetoric：修辞说法。

43 your writers：the authorities. your 系泛指。 **consent**：agree. *ipse*〈拉丁语〉：he, himself.

47—49 abandon... woman：Touchs one 为自己所用的高雅词汇加上注脚：abandon = leave; society = company; female = woman. **the vulgar**：the speech of uneducated people.第 48 行中的 boorish、第 49 行中的 common 同此。

51 or：otherwise.

51—52 to... understanding：to put it in a way so that you may better understand. **to wit**：namely.

52—53 make... away：get rid of you. **translate**：change.

54—55 bastinado〈意大利语〉：beating with a stick. **in steel**：with a sword. **bandy... in faction**：hurl insults at each other. **o'errun**：defeat.

56 policy：strategy, scheming.

WILL. God rest you merry, sir. [*Exit*.

Enter CORIN.

COR. Our master and mistress seek you: come, away, away!

TOUCH. Trip, Audrey! trip, Audrey! I attend, I attend. [*Exeunt*.

SCENE II

—Another Part of the Forest.

Enter ORLANDO *and* OLIVER.

ORL. Is't possible that on so little acquaintance you should like her? that, but seeing, you should love her? and, loving, woo? and, wooing, she should grant? and will you persever to enjoy her?

OLI. Neither call the giddiness of it in question, the poverty of her, the small acquaintance, my sudden wooing, nor her sudden consenting; but say with me, I love Aliena; say with her, that she loves me; consent with both, that we may enjoy each other: it shall be to your good; for my father's house and all the revenue that was old Sir Rowland's will I estate upon you, and here live and die a shepherd.

ORL. You have my consent. Let your wedding be tomorrow: thither will I invite the duke and all's contented followers. Go you and prepare Aliena; for, look you, here comes my Rosalind.

Enter ROSALIND.

ROS. God save you, brother.

OLI. And you, fair sister. [*Exit*.

ROS. O! my dear Orlando, how it grieves me to see thee wear thy heart in a scarf.

ORL. It is my arm.

59 **rest you merry**：keep you happy.

62—63 **Trip**：run. **attend**：am going with you.

V.ii

1 **on...acquaintance**：after knowing her for such a short time.

2 **but**：only.

3 **wooing**：分词的逻辑主语在这里仍是"you"，而不是句子主语"she".

3—4 **grant**：consent. **persever**：persevere，go on. **enjoy**：marry.

5 **call... in question**：question，doubt. **giddiness**：impulsiveness.

7 **sudden**：swift.

8 **say...me**：agree with me when I say.

10 **revenue**：income.

11 **estate upon**：bestow on.

14—15 **all's**：all his. **contented**：乐天知命的。

18 **sister**：Oliver，like Orlando，is pretending that Ganymede is Rosalind.

20 **wear...scarf**：Orlando 以前经常说他的心受了伤，Rosalind 看见他手臂裹着绷带，故意同他开玩笑。参看英谚：wear one's heart on one's sleeve.

ROS. I thought thy heart had been wounded with the claws of a lion.

ORL. Wounded it is, but with the eyes of a lady.

ROS. Did your brother tell you how I counterfeited to swound when he showed me your handkercher?

ORL. Ay, and greater wonders than that.

ROS. O! I know where you are. Nay, 'tis true: there was never anything so sudden but the fight of two rams, and Cæsar's thrasonical brag of 'I came, saw, and overcame:' for your brother and my sister no sooner met, but they looked; no sooner looked but they loved; no sooner loved but they sighed; no sooner sighed but they asked one another the reason; no sooner knew the reason but they sought the remedy: and in these degrees have they made a pair of stairs to marriage which they will climb incontinent, or else be incontinent before marriage. They are in the very wrath of love, and they will together: clubs cannot part them.

ORL. They shall be married to-morrow, and I will bid the duke to the nuptial. But, O! how bitter a thing it is to look into happiness through another man's eyes. By so much the more shall I to-morrow be at the height of heart-heaviness, by how much I shall think my brother happy in having what he wishes for.

ROS. Why, then, to-morrow I cannot serve your turn for Rosalind?

ORL. I can live no longer by thinking.

ROS. I will weary you then no longer with idle talking. Know of me then,—for now I speak to some purpose,—that I know you are a gentleman of good conceit. I speak not this that you should bear a good opinion of my knowledge, insomuch I say I know you are; neither do I labour for a greater esteem than may in some little measure draw a belief from you, to do

26 swound：swoon.

28 where you are：what you mean（指 Oliver 与 Celia 相爱）。

28—31 there...overcame：Rosalind 举出两个进展神速的例子：一是公羊打架可以一触即发；二是恺撒的傲语，寥寥三个词概括整个过程。

30 thrasonlical：Thraso 式的，i.e. boastful. Thraso 是罗马剧作家 Terence（泰伦斯，公元前 190—前 159）所写拉丁文 Eunuchus 剧中惯于自我吹嘘的士兵。

30—31 "I...overcame，"恺撒于公元前 47 年以五天时间平息黑海一带叛乱后送回罗马的信，拉丁原文是：Veni，vidi，vici.

35 degrees：stages.

37 第一个 incontinent 意为 immediately，第二个 incontinent 意为 unable to restrain the passions.

38 wrath：passionate ardour. **will**：must be.

40 bid：invite.

42—44 By so much the more...by how much I shall think：越是想到……越是……。

46—47 serve...for：act as.

48 thinking：imagination，illusion.

50 know of：learn from.

50—51 to...purpose：seriously.

52 conceit：intelligence，understanding. **that**：so that，in order that.

53 knowledge：intelligence.

53—54 insomuch：because. **you are**：you are a gentleman of good conceit.

54 labour for a great esteem than...：try to get a greater esteem than is necessary that.

55 draw a belief from you：persuade you to believe in me.

yourself good, and not to grace me. Believe then, if you please, that I can do strange things. I have since I was three year old, conversed with a magician, most profound in his art and yet not damnable. If you do love Rosalind so near the heart as your gesture cries it out, when your brother marries Aliena, shall you marry her. I know into what straits of fortune she is driven; and it is not impossible to me, if it appear not inconvenient to you, to set her before your eyes to-morrow, human as she is, and without any danger.

ORL. Speakest thou in sober meanings?

ROS. By my life, I do; which I tender dearly, though I say I am a magician. Therefore, put you in your best array; bid your friends; for if you will be married tomorrow, you shall; and to Rosalind, if you will. Look, here comes a lover of mine, and a lover of hers.

Enter SILVIUS *and* PHEBE.

PHE. Youth, you have done me much ungentleness,
To show the letter that I writ to you.

ROS. I care not if I have: It is my study
To seem despiteful and ungentle to you.
You are there follow'd by a faithful shepherd:
Look upon him, love him; he worships you.

PHE. Good shepherd, tell this youth what 'tis to love.

SIL. It is to be all made of sighs and tears; And so am I for Phebe.

PHE. And I for Ganymede.

ORL. And I for Rosalind.

ROS. And I for no woman.

SIL. It is to be all made of faith and service; And so am I for Phebe.

56 **grace** (v.t.): honour.

58 **conversed**: associated.

59 **damnable**: i.e. for involving dealings with the devil.中世纪认为魔术有两种:一善一恶。

60 **near the heart**: sincerely. **gesture**: behaviour. **cries it out**: proclaims.

62 **straits of fortune**: misfortunes.

63 **impossible to me**: impossible for me.

64 **inconvenient**: inappropriate.

65 **human...danger**: 意为 Rosalind 将亲身出现,不是魔鬼假扮,不会引起的危险巫术。

66 **sober**: serious.

67 **which**: 指 my life. **tender dearly**: value highly.

69 **array**: dress. **bid**: invite.

70 **will**: want to.

74 **show**: make public. **writ**: wrote.

75 **study**: intention.

76 **despiteful**: scornful.

PHE. And I for Ganymede.

ORL. And I for Rosalind.

ROS. And I for no woman.

SIL. It is to be all made of fantasy,
All made of passion, and all made of wishes;
All adoration, duty, and observance;
All humbleness, all patience, and impatience;
All purity, all trial, all obeisance;
And so am I for Phebe.

PHE. And so am I for Ganymede.

ORL. And so am I for Rosalind.

ROS. And so am I for no woman.

PHE. [*To* ROSALIND.] If this be so, why blame you me to love you?

SIL. [*To* PHEBE.] If this be so, why blame you me to love you?

ORL. If this be so, why blame you me to love you?

ROS. Why do you speak to, 'Why blame you me to love you?'

ORL. To her that is not here, nor doth not hear.

ROS. Pray you, no more of this; 'tis like the howling of Irish wolves against the moon . [*To* SILVIUS] I will help you, if I can: [*To* PHEBE.] I would love you, if I could. To-morrow meet me all together. [*To* PHEBE] I will marry you, if ever I marry woman, and I' ll be married to-morrow: [*To* ORLANDO.] I will satisfy you , if ever I satisfied man , and you shall be married to-morrow: [*To* SILVIUS.] I will content you, if what pleases you contents you, and you shall be married to-morrow. [*To* ORLANDO.] As you love Rosalind, meet. [*To* SILVIUS.] As you love Phebe, meet: and as I love no woman, I'll meet. So, fare you well: I have left you commands.

SIL. I'll not fail, if I live.

93 **observanee**：respect.

95 **trial**：endurance. **obeisance**：obedience.

101 **to love you**：for loving you.

108—109 **howling...moon**：①徒然的吠叫；②月亮象征伊丽莎白女王；爱尔兰狼象征爱尔兰抗英的"叛徒"。 **against**：at.

PHE. Nor I,

ORL. Nor I. [*Exeunt*.

SCENE III

—Another Part of the Forest.

Enter TOUCHSTONE *and* AUDREY.

TOUCH. To-morrow is the joyful day, Audrey; to-morrow will we be married.

AUD. I do desire it with all my heart, and I hope it is no dishonest desire to desire to be a woman of the world. Here come two of the banished duke's pages.

Enter two Pages.

FIRST PAGE. Well met, honest gentleman.

TOUCH. By my troth, well met. Come, sit, sit, and a song.

SEC. PAGE. We are for you: sit i' the middle.

FIRST PAGE. Shall we clap into't roundly, without hawking or spitting, or saying we are hoarse, which are the only prologues to a bad voice?

SEC. PAGE. I'faith: i'faith; and both in a tune, like two gipsies on a horse.

SONG

It was a lover and his lass.
  With a hey. and a ho, and a hey nonino,
That o'er the green corn-field did pass.
  In the spring time, the only pretty ring time,
When birds do sing, hey ding a ding, ding;
Sweet lovers love the spring.
Between the acres of the rye,
  With a hey, and a ho, and a hey nonino,
These pretty country folks would lie,
  In the spring time, &c.
This carol they began that hour,

V.iii

4 **dishonest**：improper.

4—5 **woman of the world**：married woman.

7 **well met**：glad to meet you.

9 **for you**：ready to sarisfy you. **sit i'the middle**：参见歌谣：Hey diddle,diddle,Fool in the middle.

10 **clap...roundly**：strike into it (the song) directly.

11 **hawking**：clearing the throat.

13 **in a tune**：sing in unison.

16 **hey...nonino**：hey 这个词并无意义，只是音调合拍，便于歌唱。第 22 行中 hey...ding 同此。

18 **ring time**：time for exchanging wedding-rings.

21 **rye**：裸麦(当时是做面包的原料)。

24 **&c.**：表示其余部分与第一段相应部分歌词相同，故省略。

With a hey, and a ho, and a hey nonino;
How that a life was but a flower
In the spring time, &c.
And therefore take the present time,
With a hey, and a ho, and a hey nonino,
For love is crowned with the prime
In the spring time, &c.

TOUCH. Truly, young gentlemen, though there was no great matter in the ditty, yet the note was very untuneable.

FIRST PAGE. You are deceived, sir: we kept time; we lost not our time.

TOUCH. By my troth, yes; I count it but time lost to hear such a foolish song . God be wi' you ; and God mend your voices! Come, Audrey.

[*Exeunt*.

SCENE IV

—*Another Part of the Forest*.

Enter DUKE SENIOR, AMIENS, JAQUES, ORLANDO, OLIVER, *and* CELIA.

DUKE S. Dost thou believe, Orlando, that the boy Can do all this that he hath promised?

ORL. I sometimes do believe, and sometimes do not;
As those that fear they hope, and know they fear.

Enter ROSALIND, SILVIUS. *and* PHEBE.

ROS. Patience once more, whiles our compact is urg'd.
[*To the* DUKE.] You say, if I bring in your Rosalind, You will bestow her on Orlando here?

DUKE S. That would I, had I kingdoms to give

29 **take**: seize.

31 **the prime**: perfection.

34 **matter**: meaning. **ditty**: words of a song. **note**: music.

35 **untuneable**: inharmonious.

36 **deceived**: mistaken.

38 **yes**: yes, you did lose (waste) your time. **but**: just. **time lost**: waste of time.

V.iv

6—7 **compact**: agreement. **urg'd**: put forward.

with her.

ROS. [*To* ORLANDO.] And you say, you will have her when I bring her?

ORL. That would I, were I of all kingdoms king.

ROS. [*To* PHEBE.] You say, that you'll marry me, if I be willing?

PHE. That will I, should I die the hour after.

ROS. But if you do refuse to marry me,
You'll give yourself to this most faithful shepherd?

PHE. So is the bargain.

ROS.[*To* SILVIUS.] You say, that you'll have Phebe, if she will?

SIL. Though to have her and death were both one thing.

ROS. I have promis'd to make all this matter even.
Keep you your word, O duke, to give your daughter;
You yours, Orlando, to receive his daughter;
Keep your word, Phebe, that you'll marry me,
Or else, refusing me, to wed this shepherd;
Keep your word, Silvius, that you'll marry her,
If she refuse me: and from hence I go,
To make these doubts all even.

[*Exeunt* ROSALIND *and* CELIA.

DUKE S. I do remember in this shepherd boy
Some lively touches of my daughter's favour.

ORL. My lord, the first time that I ever saw him,
Methought he was a brother to your daughter;
But, my good lord, this boy is forest-born,
And hath been tutor'd in the rudiments
Of many desperate studies by his uncle,
Whom he reports to be a great magician,
Obscured in the circle of this forest.

25 **even**：smooth；make even（意为 settle）。

32 **doubts**：uncertainties；questions.

35 **lively**：lifelike. **favour**：appearance.

37 **Methought**：it seems to me I thought.

39 **tutor'd**：taught.

40 **desperate**：dangerous.

42 **Obscured**：hidden. **circle**：①area；②魔术师画的圈。

Enter TOUCHSTONE *and* AUDREY.

JAQ. There is, sure, another flood toward, and these couples are coming to the ark. Here comes a pair of very strange beasts, which in all tongues are called fools.

TOUCH. Salutation and greeting to you all!

JAQ. Good my lord, bid him welcome. This is the motley-minded gentleman that I have so often met in the forest: he hath been a courtier, he swears.

TOUCH. If any man doubt that, let him put me to my purgation. I have trod a measure; I have flattered a lady; I have been politic with my friend, smooth with mine enemy; I have undone three tailors; I have had four quarrels, and like to have fought one.

JAQ. And how was that ta'en up?

TOUCH. Faith, we met, and found the quarrel was upon the seventh cause.

JAQ. How seventh cause? Good my lord, like this fellow.

DUKE S. I like him very well.

TOUCH. God 'ild you, sir; I desire you of the like. I press in here, sir, amongst the rest of the country copulatives, to swear, and to forswear, according as marriage binds and blood breaks. A poor virgin, sir, an ill-favoured thing, sir, but mine own: a poor humour of mine, sir, to take that that no man else will. Rich honesty dwells like a miser, sir, in a poor house, as your pearl in your foul oyster.

DUKE S. By my faith, he is very swift and sententious.

TOUCH. According to the fool's bolt, sir, and such dulcet diseases.

JAQ. But, for the seventh cause; how did you find the quarrel on the seventh cause?

43—44 flood...ark：典出《圣经·旧约·创世记》第6—8章。上帝降洪水之前通知诺亚造方舟，将有血肉的活物成对带进方舟躲避洪水。Jaques看到一对对青年即将成婚，故云。 **toward**：coming. **ark**：Noah's ark（诺亚方舟）。

48 motley-minded：with a mind full of mixed ideas（头脑念头杂乱的）。motley本意是各种杂色的布拼成。

50—52 put...purgation：give me the opportunity of clearing myself from accusation (of falsehood). **measure**：slow，stately dance.

52 politic：cunning.

52—53 smooth：polite.这里莎士比亚对宫廷中达官贵人进行讽刺，他们处世行事往往与常人相反。 **undone**：ruined (by no paying their bills).

54 like...one：almost had to fight a duel (to settle one of the quarrels).

55 ta'en up：settled.

57 the seventh cause：见下。

58 How：what do you mean by.

61 'ild：yield的缩写；reward.这里Touchstone在对公爵说话。

61—62 desire...like：wish you do the same.这里Touchstone在对Jaques说话。 **press**：push (my way).

62—63 copulatives：people about to marry. **swear...forswear**：起誓，然后毁誓。

64 blood breaks：lust breaks marriage. **A...virgin**：指Audrey. **ill-favoured**：plain.

65 poor humour：humble fancy.

66 that that：her whom. **Rich honesty**：precious chastity.

69—70 swift：quick-witted. **sentientious**：full of epigrams.

71—72 fool's bolt：出自谚语A fool's bolt (arrow) is soon shot（"愚人箭发得快"，意为讲话不假思索）。 **dulcet diseases**：pleasant (sweet) weaknesses.

TOUCH. Upon a lie seven times removed:—bear your body more seeming, Audrey:—as thus, sir. I did dislike the cut of a certain courtier's beard: he sent me word, if I said his beard was not cut well, he was in the mind it was: this is called 'the retort courteous.' If I sent him word again, it was not well cut, he would send me word, he cut it to please himself: this is call'd the 'quip modest.' If again it was not well cut, he disabled my judgment: this is called the 'reply churlish.' If again, it was not well cut, he would answer, I spake not true: this is called the 'reproof valiant:' if again, it was not well cut, he would say, I lie: this is called the 'countercheck quarrelsome': and so to the 'lie circumstantial,' and the 'lie direct.'

JAQ. And how oft did you say his beard was not well cut?

TOUCH. I durst go no further than the 'lie Circumstantial,' nor he durst not give me the 'lie direct;' and so we measured swords and parted.

JAQ. Can you nominate in order now the degrees of the lie?

TOUCH. O sir, we quarrel in print; by the book, as you have books for good manners: I will name you the degrees. The first, the 'retort courteous;' the second, the 'quip modest;' the third, the reply churlish;' the fourth, the 'reproof valiant;' the fifth, the 'countercheck quarrelsome;' the sixth, the 'lie with circumstance;' the seventh, the 'lie direct.' All these you may avoid but the lie direct; and you may avoid that too, with an 'if.' I knew when seven justices could not take up a quarrel; but when the parties were met themselves, one of them thought but of an 'if,' as: 'If you said so, then I said so;' and they shook hands and swore brothers. Your 'if' is the only peace-maker; much virtue in 'if.'

75 **lie...removed**：七次避免说对方在撒谎(因为明确说对方撒谎便会引起决斗)。

76 **seeming**：seemly.

76—77 **dislike**：find fault with. **cut**：shape.

79 **in the mind**：of the opinion that.

79—80 **retort courteous**：有礼貌的反驳。

82 **quip modest**：有分寸的回敬。

83 **disabled**：disparaged；denied.

84 **'reply churlish'**：粗暴的答复。

85 **spake...true**：did not speak the truth.

85—86 **reproof valiant**：大胆的指责。

87 **'countercheek quarrelsome'**：挑衅的反击。

88 **'lie circumstantial'**：间接指称撒谎。 **'lie direet'**：直接指称撒谎。

92 **durst**：dared.

93 **measured swords**：按照当时惯例，双方决斗前要比量剑的长度，彼此一致。

94 **nominate**：name. **in order**：依次。

96 **in print**：according to what is printed (the book of rules).

103 **avoid**：avoid fighting over.

104 **justices**：magistrates. **take up**：settle.

105 **but**：except.

106 **thought but of**：simply thought of. **but**：only.

106—107 **If...so**：用了 if，便排除了直接的指责或挑衅，争吵也容易被看成是因误解而起。 **swore**：pledged to be.

JAQ. Is not this a rare fellow, my lord? he's as good at any thing, and yet a fool.

DUKE S. He uses his folly like a stalking-horse, and under the presentation of that he shoots his wit.

Enter HYMEN, *leading* ROSALIND, *in woman's clothes*, *and* CELIA.

Still Music.

Hym. Then is there mirth in heaven.
When earthly things made even
Atone together.
Good duke, receive thy daughter;
Hymen from heaven brought her;
Yea, brought her hither,
That thou mightst join her hand with his,
Whose heart within her bosom is.

ROS. [*To* DUKE S.] To you I give myself, for I am yours.
[*To* ORLANDO.] To you I give myself, for I am yours.

DUKE S. If there be truth in sight, you are my daughter.

ORL. If there be truth in sight, you are my Rosalind.

PHE. If sight and shape be true,
Why then, my love adieu!

ROS. [*To* DUKE S.] I'll have no father, if you be not he.
[*To* ORLANDO.] I'll have no husband, if you be not he:
[*To* PHEBE.] Nor ne'er wed woman, if you be not she.

Hym. Peace, ho! I bar confusion:
'Tis I must make conclusion
Of these most strange events:
Here's eight that must take hands

109 rare：splendid.

111—112 stalking-horse：猎手躲在它背后以便偷偷接近猎物的掩蔽马(用布等制成的马形掩蔽体)；烟幕。 **presentation of that**：appearance of foolishness. **shoot... wit**：attack people with his cleverness.

114 mirth：joy.

115 made even：settled smoothly，过去分词短语作 things 的定语。

116 Atone (v.i.)：unite.此词由 at 与 one 两个词组成。

118 Hymen ：罗马神话中司人间婚姻的神(god of marriage).

120 his：指 Orlando's.

121 Whose：Rosalind's.当时诗人常说相爱的人成婚会交换心脏，女方的心在男方胸中，反之亦然。

125 If...sight：If what I see is true.

128 my...adieu：goodbye to my love.

132 Peace：silence. **bar**：forbid.

133 conclusion：settlement.

To join in Hymen's bands,
If truth holds true contents.

[*To* ORLANDO *and* ROSALIND.] You and you no cross shall part:
[*To* OLIVER *and* CELIA.] You and you are heart in heart:
[*To* PHEBE.] You to his love must accord,
Or have a woman to your lord:
[*To* TOUCHSTONE *and* AUDREY.] You and you are sure together,
As the winter to foul weather.
Whiles a wedlock hymn we sing,
Feed yourselves with questioning,
That reason wonder may diminish,
How thus we met, and these things finish.

SONG

Wedding is great Juno's crown:
O blessed bond of board and bed!
'Tis Hymen peoples every town;
High wedlock then be honoured.
Honour, high honour, and renown,
To Hymen, god of every town!

DUKE S. O my dear niece! welcome thou art to me:
Even daughter, welcome in no less degree.
Phe. [*To* SILVIUS.] I will not eat my word, now thou art mine;
Thy faith my fancy to thee doth combine.

Enter JAQUES DE BOYS.

Jaq. de B. Let me have audience for a word or two:

136 **Hymen's bands**：bonds of marriage.

137 If, now that you know the truth, you are contented (with your partner). **contents**：满意，重音在第二音节；抽象名词用复数。

142 **accord**：agree to accept.

143 **to ... lord**：as your husband.

144 **sure**：tightly bound.

146 **foul**：stormy.

147 **wedlock hymn**：wedding song.

148 **Feed**：satisfy. **questioning**：asking each other questions；conversation.

149 **That**：so that. **roason**：knowing the truth. **wonder**：diminish 的宾语。

152 **Juno's crown**：the best thing Juno can offer.Juno 是罗马神话中主神 Jupiter 的妻子，司人间婚姻。

153 **bond...bed**：婚姻的契约。字面意思 board 指同食，bed 指共寝。

154 **peoples** (v.t.)：who stocks...with people (inhabitants).

155 **High**：solemn.

160 **Even daughter**：as though you were my daughter.

162 Your faithfulness binds my love to you.

I am the second son of old Sir Rowland,
That bring these tidings to this fair assembly.
Duke Frederick, hearing how that every day
Men of great worth resorted to this forest,
Address'd a mighty power, which were on foot
In his own conduct, purposely to take
His brother here and put him to the sword:
And to the skirts of this wild wood he came,
Where, meeting with an old religious man,
After some question with him, was converted
Both from his enterprise and from the world;
His crown bequeathing to his banish'd brother,
And all their lands restor'd to them again
That were with him exil'd. This to be true,
I do engage my life.

DUKE S. Welcome, young man;
Thou offer'st fairly to thy brothers' wedding:
To one, his lands withheld; and to the other
A land itself at large, a potent dukedom.
First, in this forest, let us do those ends
That here were well begun and well begot;
And after, every of this happy number
That have endur'd shrewd days and nights with us,
Shall share the good of our returned fortune,
According to the measure of their states.
Meantime, forget this new-fall'n dignity,
And fall into our rustic revelry.
Play, music! and you, brides and bridegrooms all,
With measure heap'd in joy, to the measures fall.

JAQ. Sir, by your patience. If I heard you rightly,
The duke hath put on a religious life,
And thrown into neglect the pompous court?

JAQ. DE B. He hath.

JAQ. To him will I: Out of these convertites

167 **these tidings**: the following news. **fair assembly**: good company.

170 **Address'd**: raised. **power**: army.

171 **In... conduct** : under his personal command. **purposely**: with the purpose. **take**: capture.

172 **put... sword**: kill him.

173 **skirts**: outskirts.

175—176 **question**: conversation. **converted... world**: 悔悟过去做错了事,决定停止他的这次行动,谢绝人世。

179—180 **This... life**: 我以生命担保,我所说的是实话。 **engage**: pledge.

182 **offer'st fairly**: bring handsome gifts.

183 **To one... withheld**: to Oliver, whose lands were taken from him. **to the other**: to Orlando,他成了王位继承人。

184 **A land... large**: an entire country. **potent**: mighty.

185 **do those ends**: finish those things.

186 **begot**: brought about; generated.

187 **number**: assembly; company.

188 **shrewd**: hard.

190 **measure**: degree, level. **states**: ranks.

191 **new-fall'n dignity**: newly-acquired high position.

194 **measure heap'd in**: cup full of. **measures**: : dancing. **fall**: join in.

195 **patience**: permission.

199 **will I**: I shall go. **out of**: from. **convertites**: religious converts,皈依者。

There is much matter to be heard and learn'd.
[*To* DUKE S.] You to your former honour I bequeath;
Your patience and your virtue well deserves it.
[*To* ORLANDO.] You to a love that your true faith doth merit:
[*To* OLIVER.] You to your land, and love, and great allies:
[*To* SILVIUS.] You to a long and well-deserved bed:
[*To* TOUCHSTONE.] And you to wrangling; for thy loving voyage
Is but for two months victual'd. So, to your pleasures; I am for other than for dancing measures.

DUKE S. Stay, Jaques, stay.

JAQ. To see no pastime, I: —what you would have I'll stay to know at your abandon'd cave. [*Exit.*

DUKE S. Proceed, proceed: we will begin these rites,
As we do trust they'll end, in true delights.
[*A dance. Exeunt.*

205—206 **allies**：friends.

207 **long**：长久享用的。

208—209 **wrangling**：quarrelling. **loving voyage**：爱情的航程。

210 **victual'd**：provided with food.

213 **pastime**：entertainment. **would have**：want to know.

215 **rites**：marriage ceremonies.

EPILOGUE

Spoken by ROSALIND

It is not the fashion to see the lady the epilogue: but it is no more unhandsome than to see the lord the prologue. If it be true that good wine needs no bush, 'tis true that a good play needs no epilogue; yet to good wine they do use good bushes, and good plays prove the better by the help of good epilogues. What a case am I in then, that am neither a good epilogue, nor cannot insinuate with you in the behalf of a good play! I am not furnished like a beggar, therefore to beg will not become me: my way is, to conjure you; and I'll begin with the women. I charge you, O women! for the love you bear to men, to like as much of this play as please you: and I charge you, O men! for the love you bear to women, — as I perceive by your simpering none of you hate them,—that between you and the women, the play may please. If I were a woman I would kiss as many of you as had beards that pleased me, complexions that liked me, and breaths that I defied not; and, I am sure, as many as have good beards, or good faces, or sweet breaths, will, for my kind offer, when I make curtsy, bid me farewell.

[*Exeunt*.

EPILOGUE(收场白)

1 lady：女主角。宾语和补语间省略 as. **epilegue**：说收场白的人。

2 unhandsome：unfitting. **lord**：男女角。

2—3 prologue：说开场白的人。 **bush**：酒店门前所挂的一圈常青藤，用作广告标志。

6 case：situation.

7—8 insinuate：plead. **in the behalf of**：on behalf of.

9 furnished：dressed.

10 become：suit. **conjure**：charm.

14—15 simpering：smirking, smiling. **I...woman**：当时女角均系由男孩扮演。

18 liked：pleased. **defied**：disliked.

21 bid me farewell：i.e. by clapping.

图书在版编目(CIP)数据

皆大欢喜/(英)莎士比亚(Shakespeare, W.)著;罗志野,李德荣注释.—北京:商务印书馆,2014(2016.3 重印)
(莎翁戏剧经典)
ISBN 978-7-100-09953-0

Ⅰ.①皆… Ⅱ.①莎… ②罗… ③李… Ⅲ.①英语—语言读物 ②剧本—英国—中世纪 Ⅳ.①H319.4:I

中国版本图书馆 CIP 数据核字(2013)第 095849 号

所有权利保留。
未经许可,不得以任何方式使用。

莎翁戏剧经典
JIĒ DÀ HUĀN XǏ
皆 大 欢 喜
〔英〕威廉·莎士比亚 著
罗志野 李德荣 注释

商务印书馆出版
(北京王府井大街36号 邮政编码 100710)
商务印书馆发行
北京冠中印刷厂印刷
ISBN 978-7-100-09953-0

2014年8月第1版 开本 787×1092 1/32
2016年3月北京第2次印刷 印张 6⅞ 插页 1

定价:23.00 元

ngen walking by Closer Wish I was a sinking Changing to other days Every

thing I have to beg I'd be closer closer to you Closer got to get closer closer to you

and that Even a tail To satisfied Just being round your leg When I am dream

ken walking Changing decorate your life Closer closer closer to you Closer get

a white hat Draped down your head When you feel the time was right I'd

you Closer closer closer to round your back Right next to your bed Trying to mak

y Closer closer closer to you If I had my wishes If I had my way I'll be all the

Wish I was a sinking Changing to other days Every

... to you Closer got to get closer closer to you

...that I'm a girl to satisfied Just being round your leg When I'm dream

...a wedding Hanging from your lips Closer closer closer to you Closer ...

...a naked idea Draped down your front When you feel the time was right I ...

you Closer closer closer to round your bed Right next to your den Trying to ...

...g Closer closer closer to you If I had my wishes If I had my way I'd be all th...

...on you walking by Closer Wish I was a stocking Clinging to your thighs Ever...

...ather I have to beg I'd be closer closer to you Closer got to get closer closer to you